SHADOWS ON THE ROAD

LIFE AT THE HEART OF THE PELOTON, FROM US POSTAL TO TEAM SKY

Michael Barry

FABER & FABER

First published in 2014
by Faber & Faber Ltd
Bloomsbury House
74–77 Great Russell Street
London WC1B 3DA

Typeset by Faber & Faber Ltd
Printed in England by CPI Group (UK) Ltd, Croydon, CRO 4YY

PHOTO SECTION CREDITS
Page 1: BOTTOM, Mike Barry. Page 2: *both*, Ralph Lapp. Page 3: BOTTOM, Mike Barry.
Page 5: © Graham Watson. Page 6: TOP, © Doug Pensinger, 2005 Getty Images.
BOTTOM, *left and right*, © Greg Parks. Page 7: TOP, © Scott Mitchell. BOTTOM, ©
Bryn Lennon, 2010 Getty Images. Page 8: TOP, Ian Austen. BOTTOM, Walter Lai

*Every effort has been made to trace or contact all copyright holders.
The publishers would be pleased to rectify at the earliest opportunity
any errors or omissions brought to their notice.*

A CIP record for this book
is available from the British Library

ISBN 978–0–571–29771–9

FSC
www.fsc.org
MIX
Paper from
responsible sources
FSC® C101712

2 4 6 8 10 9 7 5 3 1

For my family

PROLOGUE

The phone rang at the arranged time. The caller ID matched the number on the email. This was the call I had anticipated for nine years. One I knew would forever change my life. It rang twice. I answered as I turned down the radio. My wife drove, and I sat in the passenger seat of the minivan, with our children in the back. A dinner date had been planned with another family on the Toronto waterfront.

Only a few hours earlier, I had announced my retirement from professional cycling. For two years I had considered whether or not I should stop but with time the decision became easier. Weeks on end away from my family, the crashes, the injuries and the resulting anxiety had become too much. But I kept going, as I wanted to be sure I was making the right decision and I feared giving up a passion and a dream I had pursued since I was a small boy. I loved being on my bike, but the demands of the job had eroded my will and crushed my body.

Soon after publicly announcing this would be my last season and the coming races that weekend in Quebec City and Montreal my final races in Canada, I started receiving emails of congratulations for a long career racing at the highest level. Then there had been that email requesting a phone conversation.

The car seats held the warmth of the hot summer day and the air conditioning blasted as it battled to lower the temperature. Our boys had just finished a day at summer camp, and I had been training all day, my final hard session before the races on the weekend. The visible veins in my legs, a sign of my fitness, the hard training session and the dehydrating heat, lined the thin skin like the rural roads on a map of France. The scar on my arm from recent surgeries after two heavy crashes had turned red from hours under the sun, and the titanium plate beneath the scar made it tender to touch. Six weeks after the last surgery, the broken bone still ached. My forearm bulged, slightly swollen from a screw head rubbing on tissue. Like a cat licking a wound I massaged the scar while I held the phone between my shoulder and ear.

The car descended into the valley, along the Don River. The hill we drove down, I had ridden up daily as a boy, timing each ascent. Back then, two minutes and forty-eight seconds was my fastest ascent. The valley hadn't changed much in twenty years. There were a few new buildings on the ridges. The landfill where motocross riders once tore around had grown into a green park where dog walkers strolled with their pets. The old pulp and paper mill and the skeleton of an abandoned housing project had been ripped down, and the chemical aromas of 1970s and '80s industry that wafted off the river had been replaced by more natural scents. But otherwise it was all the same. On the bike, I often pass spots I have seen since I was a boy. I even recognise markings on the road, unchanged in decades. Our lives take turns, we age, we leave and we return, we win and we lose, but many of those spots remain identical and somehow provide comfort. On the phone, knowing nothing in my life would ever be the same, I looked out the window at the valley that had been a part of me since I was a boy, and I felt oddly calm. My life was about to take a direction that I had fought to avoid, yet I knew I would inevitably face it. I'm not sure we can ever escape our lies, errors and sins. Even if they don't become public, they will haunt us and devour us from within. There was emptiness in my stomach and nervousness in my voice as I answered the call, but these symptoms had not been triggered by fear of the consequences. I was willing to accept the consequences. I was concerned about the complexities that I didn't yet know how to handle. I had no idea how it would all unfold, but I had faith that good could come, as it always does, regardless of how challenging the path.

The conversation was short. Bill Bock, the lead lawyer in the United States Anti-Doping Agency (USADA) investigation, politely introduced himself. He was calm, his words were succinct, yet friendly. Dede put a movie on for the boys, to keep them occupied and quieter while I was on the phone. In the background Lightning McQueen chattered and revved his engine through the speakers. Mr Bock explained that he knew I rode for the US Postal Service cycling team, and understood I was involved in the use of performance-enhancing substances. He listed the substances, erythropoeitin (EPO), growth hormone and testosterone, and said he was told I had used them from 2003 to 2006, the years that I rode for the team. I said little, other than perhaps a yes or an okay. He asked if I would like to co-operate in their investigation and if they could meet me in the next few days. It was my choice either to co-operate or to continue to lie. I agreed to testify, but explained I was scheduled to race in Montreal. They could meet me there. Mr Bock then explained that the other riders involved had lawyers to represent them, and that I might want to contact one as well.

I had doped during a period of my career and had used the substances Mr Bock listed. To avoid being caught, I had lied. When an ex-teammate, Floyd Landis, publicly said that we had shared EPO, I denied the claim and called him a liar.

The investigation into Lance Armstrong, my ex-teammate, and the US Postal team had been ongoing for two years, beginning shortly after Floyd admitted to doping and made allegations against the team. This was the first time I had been called for testimony directly by the US agencies involved. With a looming deadline, it was now the final stretch in their investigation.

The harbour was calm. A few boats sailed near the port. Two kayakers paddled under a bridge and into a channel. The late summer sun was still hot, but there weren't many people by the water. The club where we'd arranged to meet our friends was a short boat ride from the harbour, on a small island. The ride on the ferry calmed me. Our boys fought to sit on the boat's benches. They bounced in their seats and laughed with their friends as we pulled away from the pier. We were only a few hundred metres from the heart of the bustling city, but the island was serene, and the hum of city traffic faded under the squawk of the gulls, the lap of the waves and the rumble of the ferry's diesel engine. With my family and our friends, the turmoil inside my head subsided. I wanted to hold on to this moment until I knew how to deal with the future.

Like all of us, I could never have predicted the path of my life. As children, we set off in pursuit of our dreams. Some of us achieve them, others abandon them for more immediate goals. Sometimes we give in too easily to the mundane routines, the pursuit of wealth, the acquisition of chattels and the expectations of a society in which the only success is victory and the only distinction is performance. I gave in many times to the forces of conformity. But there was always an even greater desire that drove me further.

I'd spent my life playing, training and racing on a bicycle.

I was fortunate to have had the opportunity to pursue a child-hood passion. I chased my dreams. I loved being on a bike, and I made a living doing it. Cycling took me all over the world. I travelled year-round, often to exotic places. I had my parents' unwavering support when I was a boy and later, when I rode for the leading professional teams in the world. Through my career I earned a reputation as a trusted domestique – support rider – and I helped many top cyclists as they raced to victory in the most important professional competitions of the season.

A love of riding, the liberty of going distances at speed, alone or with friends, pushed me to get back on my bike when, per-haps, I should have given up. I'd felt the same emotion on the bike today as I'd felt as a boy when I first learned to ride. That emotion carried me to places I would never have imagined, drove me to do things that were wrong, crushed me, matured me, challenged me every day, cemented relationships, and in-formed my life's pursuit.

Stepping off the ferry, my foot pressed against the step and my muscles flexed under the load. On a bike, I felt fluid. On land, I felt uncomfortable and my movements felt abrupt. In every way, I was a competitive cyclist. The cleanly shaven legs, the tan lines on my arms, legs and neck, the scars, the skeletal physique: these were the physical signs that I rode a bike. In-ternally, it was even more evident, but only to me and perhaps my family.

The boys and their friends leapt off the boat and raced ahead of us, running on the lush green grass and daring each other to run through the sprinklers. The bounce in their strides was everything mine lacked, having been drained by my training sessions. Watching them run in circles, touch the water and leap back to avoid soaking their clothing, I wondered how I would tell them, and how they would deal with knowing their father had cheated. The people closest to me would be the hardest to tell. I wondered how they would react and if they would ever forgive me. I hoped that, through my testimony and through the USADA investigation, these kids would never face the same realities as I had or have to make the same decisions as I did if they wanted to become professional cyclists.

I still loved to ride. Racing had worn me out, but cycling had kept me going. It still does.

1

The morning drive to the airport is one we've done hundreds of times. I sit uncomfortably in the passenger's seat as José, the taxi driver, chats. He is my age, thirty-six. When I first moved to Europe to race professionally in the spring of 2002, he picked me up at the Barcelona airport and drove me 120 kilometres northwest, to my new home in Girona.

Gazing out of the window at the passing countryside, listening to him chat, I realise that all that was once foreign has become familiar. I can't place the moment when Catalonia became home. When I was a boy Europe seemed exotic, a place where I always imagined I would one day live. France, Belgium and Italy were the homes of my idols. Now as I contemplate retirement, Toronto, my birthplace, seems oddly foreign. I feel as though I'm floating in the ocean between continents, a nomad no longer attached to a culture, a country or a home.

On the way to the airport I notice the subtle changes in landscape only a local commuting to work would recognise. Whether it is early in the morning or near midnight, the conversation with José is good. Already aware if we have won or lost from the news reports, he alludes to the races but shifts topics with the next breath. He understands this is a brief escape for me, and we chat about everything else. I joke with my teammates that José has taught me to speak Spanish. It's not far from the truth.

The low January sun shines through his window. He adjusts the visor. I dig in my bag for my sunglasses. My teammate Jeremy Hunt – Jez – sits in the back, quietly. On either side of the motorway, green fields of spring crops give way to slopes which transition into tree-covered hills, and then barren peaks. Two days ago, Jez and I were in those hills, riding, pushing each other to exhaustion, recovering and then doing it again. Out there, we felt fast and strong. We pedalled the last kilometres home on an endorphin high. Now I question whether our fitness will be enough to fight the desert winds that gust and blow off the Gulf and across the Qatari peninsula. In two days, we will find out. My mind shifts away from my concerns and back to José's voice. I listen. The economy is the topic, as it is everywhere outside our insular community of expatriate cyclists. Jez hasn't said a word. His mind is on the race. I can feel it.

We're both veterans and this is likely our last season of racing. We want to retire on our own terms. Too many riders squeeze every last ounce out of their bodies to continue for one or two more seasons. Their names fade with their results. Their bodies become worn with the crashes and kilometres, effects I'm already starting to feel. The drive to extend their careers comes at the sacrifice of their families. Unable to find a life outside of cycling, a rider gives up everything else for the professional's existence. His routine brings comfort. He'll move with, and within, his nomadic family until he is no longer fit enough to follow the frantic rhythm of its world. After that, he is left alone, unable to perform but without roots or a home. My fear is that I will be trapped, without the ability to make the transition after a lifetime on a bike. Since I was a boy, I always knew that my dream job had its limits.

In conversations with the younger riders at the dinner table, the generation gap is now noticeable. Not long ago I was one of them. Now, with a family and a lifetime of racing experience, my perspective has changed. With each passing year, the veterans on the team find they have more in common with the staff than with their younger teammates.

Pedalling through the countryside or lying awake in a shared hotel room, Jez and I consider our options, reflect on our past, and prepare for the future. But in the taxi, on our way to the first race of our last season, our thoughts are stuck on the imminent start line.

After packing my bag for thousands of races, I still fear I've forgotten something. I then ask Jez to check my carry-on bag in the back seat for my passport. He finds it. It isn't the fear of forgetting something that makes me anxious; it's everything else. No matter how well trained we are, we can't control our competition, the climate, the race or the crashes. The unknowns are haunting. They often keep us up at night. Until I clip into my pedals, and the race has begun, the thoughts swirl through my head. Once on the road, everything falls into place. On the bike emotions are levelled. Clarity is found with the fluidity of the pedal stroke. The emotional undulations vanish.

Jez speaks my thoughts. 'Still, after seventeen years, I get nervous when I leave home for a race. You never know how good you'll be or what will happen.' Jez has struggled during the pre-season training camps with tendonitis in his knee. The pain subsided for ten days and then returned after he did a long hard sprint while training. Just after Christmas he changed his pedals and within a day his knee was sore again. Countless hours of riding over decades have tuned our bodies. Adapting to new equipment or changes in position is now a slow, potentially painful process. Lowering a saddle a few millimetres, changing chamois in our shorts or a misaligned shoe plate can lead to months of pain if the changes aren't progressive and closely monitored. While he was unable to ride, Jez's weight ballooned.

Knowing his weight would hinder his performance he fell into a deeper downward spiral while questions mounted in his head. Every professional has been in the same situation. We find comfort in that mutual understanding and we lean on it when we're down.

Sadness sank in this morning when the taxi arrived to pick me up. I didn't feel ready to leave my family, but I also knew that, once I was on the road, my mind would turn to my job, the race. Before I left, Dede embraced me and wished me good luck. To survive the time apart, we've learned to bury emotion in routine and work. We find calm and grace outdoors, on our bikes. Accustomed to the incessant coming and going that is the norm in every cyclist's life, we no longer shed tears like we did as young lovers.

I packed my bike bag and suitcase into the trunk of José's van. As soon as we pulled away, Dede gave a quick wave, turned towards the front door and fell back into her routine. As we passed the school my sons attend, I thought of them, working in their classrooms and playing with their friends. They had their routine. And mine, built around the racing season, was also about to begin again. Countless times before the first race, riders, friends and family said to me, 'It all starts again.'

Even José's life revolves around the racing season. In 1996, my friend and ex-teammate George Hincapie picked José's name out of the phone book. George was on his way to start his first Tour de France, and he needed a drive to the airport. After that, José drove George to the airport for almost all of the Tours he rode. As he tells me now about the first trip to the airport with George, there is a tinge of pride in his voice. Like George, he was just a young adult without obligations. He tells me how he rode his motorbike at dangerous speeds, without fear. But age has made him realise the stupidity of those antics. Maturity is sobering.

Since then the number of cyclists living in Girona has ballooned from three to more than sixty. With fewer Catalan clients, José now relies on professional cyclists for income. To me, he has become a grounding point that makes Girona feel like a home. He has become a friend to chat with when I come home from races injured and a familiar face at the airport when I step out of the terminal into the sea of tourists and business people.

We speed away from Girona. For the next ten months, I will be moving relentlessly through the scenery of one country after another, always focused on a goal and a finish line. In fourteen seasons as a professional and during a lifetime spent racing a bike, I know I can't make any predictions of how it will turn out. It doesn't matter as long as I'm on my bike, moving, going.

2

As the garage door opens, a rush of cold hits my body, piercing my Lycra. The frigid air against my face jolts me, as it did when I stepped out the door of our house in central Toronto to ride to school as a boy. It brings back a flash of memory: wearing flannel pants, black brogues, a sports jacket and tie while pedalling to school on the icy Toronto streets. Twenty years later in Spain, I still feel like that kid. The bite of the cold brings life to my body. It is late December 2011, just after Christmas, and the first race I'll ride, in Qatar, is still over a month away.

I descend into town from our house on top of the mountain above Girona. A heavy layer of fog covers the valley below, enveloping the river and the buildings. Like a beacon, the cathedral's spire breaks through. There is a serene silence. The fog dampens the commuters' noise as the city comes alive below me. Above it, a bird's song is louder. The freewheel of my bicycle ticks over, like a whirling wind-up toy. As I know the descent, I fly through the corners. The air bites me harder as the speed increases. As they notice me fast approaching in their rearview mirrors, drivers pull to the right and wave me through. In the third to last hairpin turn, I cut through the fog and feel the life of the town. School kids swarm the sidewalks, animated in the early hour as they meet their friends outside the playground. Drivers patiently wait at intersections. Passing the long line of cars, I see a familiar face behind a windscreen, wave, and continue deeper into the centre of town. The roads become more congested, forcing me to snake my way through the cars, dodging side mirrors and bumpers. Scooters follow my lead until we reach a bottleneck they can't squeeze through. The road opens up, I pedal through the roundabout, jump a curb, and enter the ancient cobblestone streets of the old town.

The town square, the *plaça*, is an oasis from the traffic. Bundled in winter parkas, people sit on the terraces, soaking up the winter sun, puffing cigarettes and sipping coffee. Pigeons peck the croissant crumbs under the tables. Other birds bob around the Civil War monument in the centre of the gravel square. Men unload fish, meat and fresh produce onto trolleys from the back of their refrigerated trucks. I see the same faces each morning. Recognising them, I nod hello.

As I reach the cafe, which is tucked in the corner of the square under the stone arcade, I realise I'm late. A pile of bikes leans against its wall. Even under the dim arcade light, their carbon parts and glossy frames glisten. Through the glass doors, I can see the flurry of colour; riders are clustered around tables in their brilliantly coloured Lycra, slurping coffees and munching on pastries. Seeing me arrive, they ask for the cheque and begin pulling on hats and buckling helmets. We don't linger. The cathedral bells gong ten times. Riders grab their bikes from the pile. We clip into our pedals, the snap of the bindings echoing under the arcade. We're off to work. But our work still feels like play.

Bradley Wiggins, my teammate on the British-sponsored Team Sky, is training in Girona for the week to escape the wet and cold of England. We instinctively fall into formation as we ride out of town. On the bike, in our small group, I feel good: two Brits, Bradley and Jez, and two Canadians, Dominique Rollin and me. The four of us pair up and then move tight against the kerb. We begin to pedal a steady rhythm. Cars pass us, the occasional driver tooting his horn, and the occasional passenger craning her neck to catch a glimpse.

Since I signed a contract with Team Sky for the 2010 season, three years ago, I've spent a lot of time with Bradley both at races and in training camps. But I still have never quite figured him out. He isn't a team leader, in the literal sense, but simply the rider on our team who has the best chance of winning the Tour de France. I like being around him. We have a few similar interests. But often I wonder what he thinks of me. He is complex, introverted and hard to decipher. At ease, he'll humour the team with his impressions, his comedic routine. But he rarely laughs at himself or alludes to his own fears and weaknesses. When under pressure, he escapes to his own world.

In the 2010 Giro d'Italia, Brad stormed the opening prologue and won convincingly. After that the pressure was off. He had achieved a goal, and the rest of the three-week race became a training session for the Tour de France. At least, that was the plan. But when a rider feels good, it is easier to press on and go for the victory rather than back off and conserve. There's always a delicate balance: dig too deep and risk fatigue, relax too much and lose fitness. In an incredibly difficult Giro, Brad pushed through perhaps one day too many, finishing tired and empty. As the race wound down, he began to fade on the final mountain passes, pushing when he should have been riding at an easier tempo. The balance was lost. As we approached the Tour six weeks later, he was clearly tired. Or perhaps the pressure to perform was eating him from within. No one could tell. We, his teammates, were there to help. But, somewhat like a turtle escaping danger, he tucked himself away in the back of the team bus, his headphones on.

Almost two years later, riding through the Catalan countryside, Brad is relaxed. The initial moments of unease when we met at the cafe have dissipated into friendly chatter. He asks questions. Often, it seems he already knows the answers and is just seeking confirmation. Or maybe he's simply inquisitive. He consumes cycling history; a boyhood obsession we share and which for him has yet to abate. Over the five hours of riding our conversation shifts and turns.

As with any memorable evening with friends, I can recall the time together, but not necessarily the small details. But I do remember a short bit of our long conversation from that ride. Brad and I were considering our life away from cycling and our families. I asked him how long he would go on racing. Like most cyclists he hadn't picked an end point, but he said that he couldn't be away from home as much as the sport demanded. Home with his family was where he felt comfortable, Brad said, and he wouldn't sacrifice his family for the sport. He continued to open up, telling me how money and success had only made his life more complex. The gold medals he had won each marked another goal achieved. Others admire them as they inspire dreams, but for the victor they become an object like any other. The goal is achieved; as athletes we simply set another goal and move on to pursue it.

From those comments I understood his introversion and elusiveness. The effort of riding gives us an escape by stripping away the complexities that create anxiety. We open up, allowing others in. On the bike, we can find equilibrium, focus and tranquillity.

In a career there are moments that become resonant memories. Most of them come not from the superficial kisses on the podium or the fleeting accolades of the media and fans, but from time spent on the bike or with teammates on the terrace of a hotel. In the peloton we see hundreds of faces through a season but become well acquainted with only a few dozen. I had seen Brad at a few races during the first years of my professional career in Europe. We had nodded hello in elevators and over breakfast buffets, but our conversations never went beyond a few sentences of small talk. He was a muscular Olympic track rider with the British National Team who rode professionally with the French team Cofidis. After 2009, when he shifted his focus to the road, he stripped his body of bulky muscle and fat. He became a contender, competing against the strongest riders in the high mountains. Now, on Sky, he is our leader.

There is a moment Brad and I both recall with clarity: during the 2006 Critérium du Dauphiné Libéré, we rode together, almost silently, up Mont Ventoux. The sounds of the chains ticking over, the gears occasionally shifting and our patterned breathing all seemed in synch with our cadence. The memory is vivid.

The Dauphiné was my first race after a two-month break. I'd fallen that year in a terrifying crash in the Tour of Flanders and woke up in a hospital with two broken vertebrae and my body covered in scrapes. Fearing the risks, I swore never to race again. As a father, I owed it to my family. But time passed, I healed, and I resumed riding. I felt good again, and I was climbing better than I had all season, although in the back of my mind I questioned my choices and the culture in which I was immersed. The crash had brought clarity. I had to change the way I was living.

Knowing I was fit, the team entered me in the Dauphiné, a top-level race where teams test their riders before the Tour de France. Even though I was racing again, I wasn't certain I would continue through another season. I rode each kilometre as if it would be my last. It became a spiritual journey, which brought me back to my youth and a trip I had experienced with my father.

In 1984, when I was eight years old, my father, a keen cyclist, had taken me to France to tour the countryside on a tandem. My aunt and uncle, on another tandem, were our travelling companions. From Grenoble to Marseilles we sought out the smallest rural roads, stopped in vineyards to picnic and on beaches to swim. At night, my father would unfold the ruffled Michelin map and place it on the hotel-room bed. The route we had completed was highlighted. Before bed we would study the map to highlight the roads we would follow in the morning. Being able to pick any road to any castle or any climb was magical. It was my first introduction to France and the roads on which my heroes had raced. In the final few days of the trip, we ascended Mont Ventoux, a gigantic, barren extinct volcano in the south of France. I can recall almost every metre of the ascent. I was a boy climbing to the heavens, imagining I was leading the Tour in the yellow jersey, attacking and dropping my rivals under the baking sun. Near the summit, we stopped at the Tommy Simpson memorial, a haunting granite rock with a cyclist etched on its face that sits on the bleak slope. I already knew the story of Simpson, having read about it in the stack of magazines and books in our living room in Toronto. On his way up the mountain during the 1967 Tour de France, Simpson had collapsed. Not wanting to give up, he begged, 'On, on, on,' to his mechanic and directeur. They tried to convince him to stop, but then helped him back onto his bike. He pedalled a few strokes further, until his heart gave out, and he died.

Simpson had doped to extremes in his attempt to win the Tour, and the drugs had killed him as he raced up the mountain. Too young to understand the true tragedy, I was more intrigued by the mountain and my heroes. My father stood quietly in front of the monument where visitors had left flowers, rocks, cycling caps and water bottles in homage to their fallen idol, and took a photo of me, standing in my blue, white and black woollen jersey, my gangly legs inside slightly baggy wool tights, my scraggly hair, embraced by the serenity of the mountain. Over the years I gazed at the photo in the album, reliving the ascent. It is only now, as a father, that I understand why my father seemed so contemplative as he snapped the photo.

In the Dauphiné, twenty-two years later, as I reached the Ventoux, I relived that moment. In the race, I had accomplished my job of keeping the leaders out of the wind and in position until we arrived at the initial slopes of the climb. As a domestique, I no longer had to perform for others. I was now free to climb at my own speed. The only thing the team asked of me was to conserve energy for the coming stages. As my team leader raced on ahead, I sank into the effort. Returning to my childhood, I fell into a tempo that took me out of the race and back to my past. I rode knowing this could be my last race up the climb. Within the first few kilometres, I caught and passed Brad. As I rode by him, he moved into my slipstream and asked if he could ride with me. 'Sure,' I said. The stage contenders were already minutes ahead of us. Our goal was simply to get to the line. Together, we climbed the mythical mountain at a steady tempo, and grace fell over me.

It was no longer just a race to me, but something more. The climb, the past, and the unpredictable future took me out of the bubble in which the race moved. I was somewhere better, where I felt content and at ease, even though my heart pumped at 180 beats a minute, my legs burned as they pushed the pedals, and my lungs fought to find air as the altitude rose and oxygen thinned.

Every few minutes we passed small groups of riders who had pooled together. Occasionally a rider would move into our slipstream only to give up. As we broke through the tree line and onto the barren landscape a gusting wind hit us in the face. We pressed on. We crossed the finish line – just two names somewhere in the middle of a list of over a hundred finishers. Only we would remember our ride. Forever.

For Brad, perhaps, it was also a time he wanted to give himself to the effort and the race. Simpson had been an icon in Britain and his legend lived on as one of the most successful British professionals. As Brad led our Team Sky during the Tour in 2010, for good fortune he carried a relic of Simpson's in his back pocket: a small piece of his woollen undershirt in an airtight plastic bag.

Now, five years after our ascent of Mont Ventoux, Bradley and I ride at a consistent pace through the Garrotxa, in northern Catalonia. Midway through the five-hour ride we stop at a small cafe to warm up and refuel. The cafe stops are also a social ritual. We all look forward to them, not because we need a break, but because we can relax, eat cakes and sip coffee, adding a splash of normality to our training routine.

Fuelled by caffeine and sugar from the stop, we push the pedals with a bit more power as we snake our way out of the town and back into the lush rural landscape. Like a beautiful face with a gaze that tells a story of a tragic past, the countryside around Girona is haunting. In the solemnity of the stubbled fields, the ancient stone farmhouses and the dark humid woods, I can sense a recent history of soldiers and battles. Crosses and monuments mark the hilltops.

As we climb, the group falls silent. We focus on the increasing effort. With each training ride I feel my fitness returning. The team training camps in January will push me further and, by the end of the month, I'll be ready to race. We train for months for the first race. Progressively, our lives become increasingly monastic as the racing season nears. Like a monk's spirituality, our fitness depends on every movement, on or off the bicycle.

Reaching the Girona town sign, I can feel the weight of the ride in my legs. The wear of the ride shows on my companions' faces, which are marked with salt and now seem gaunt. The sun and road grime have darkened our skin. My hands are slightly sticky from the syrupy drink in my bottles, the energy bars, and sweat. Jez and I ride up the final climb to my house. It is three kilometres up the mountain, from the Roman city centre to the suburban neighbourhood where we live. It is relentlessly steep. We pass a school, the children yelling, laughing and chattering in the playground. Farther up, a chained dog barks at us, guarding a modern house. We're no longer putting much pressure on the pedals, but trying to spin our legs and warm down as we chat. Jez's knee has started to ache, but I've felt good and strong all day. Now I wonder whether we might have done too much. Or maybe too little? In a few days we'll be off to the team training camp in Majorca. How fit are our teammates? Will we perform as we should? Have we trained enough to begin another season?

3

We have been in Majorca for a week. I leave the hotel for a late afternoon walk with Jez, just as Brad shows up from the airport. The team has rented the entire place for six weeks. Waves of riders come and go according to their training schedule and objectives. Seeing new riders arrive after we've been there a week feels odd. The hours we pass together on our bikes bond us in a unique way. New faces momentarily throw off the balance. But within a day of riding, they'll fall into the fold.

Two riders, Bernie Eisel and Juan Antonio Flecha, ride towards the hotel, ending their long day of training. They appear drained. Their faces look thinner than they did in the morning, and they are flushed from the cold winter air, with a layer of thin grime glistening with their sweat. Their eyes are slightly bloodshot, with darker rings underneath caused by the fine road grit, exhaust and wind. Rod Ellingworth, our coach, pulls up behind them on a scooter. He is dressed as warmly as a snow-mobiler, but he looks cold. The riders have just completed a seven-hour training session in the mountains. They have spent the final hour and a half riding in the slipstream of the motor-bike to simulate the speed of a race. Training to reach their peak fitness for the early-season one-day northern European Classics, they push hard over the distance, teaching their bodies to adapt to the duration and intensity required for the races.

Jez and I had started our training day with them. We ended our session after five and a half hours. That was one and a half hours ago. It seems we have done a lot in the time they rode further: showered, eaten, answered emails, spoken with the doctors, sat in our room and listened to a few songs while we read. They've done nothing but ride. I feel guilty, as if I should have been out there with them for the extra work. Even though I know the training would have done me no good, since my goals are different from theirs, I feel the same guilt as I did when I was a boy, and only now am I learning to control it. 'More is not always better,' I tell myself. The gap is narrow between too much and too little. Most of my coaches have emphasised the need to do more work than everybody else. And my competitive spirit fuelled the need to always be better. I was told that if I wanted to win I needed to put 'miles in the bank'. The theory was based on the success of past champions, Eastern European training philosophies, and a lack of scientific evidence to teach otherwise. It does not allow for the necessary recovery that the body needs to fully gain the benefits of the hard work.

In every team there is an internal competition that extends to accumulating hours of training. The directeurs congratulate those who have done extra work, impressed by their stamina. Too often, we are overly impressed by those who perform well at camp, who have worked more during the off season, and who are ready for an early fight. When October comes, teams are always left scrounging to fill their rosters for the final races of the season, because riders are worn out, sick, or injured. Team Sky tries to be different: its directeurs have learned from past mistakes, and they apply more science than historical lore.

I know from past mistakes that more isn't always better. All of us have different race programmes, objectives and bodies. My legs ache. I'm tired. I've done the work that the coach has written on my training programme. Perhaps it is not only guilt I feel but also a tinge of jealousy. The feeling of being physically empty is fulfilling. I'm jealous I don't feel what they feel. They've reached beyond their perceived limit, worn themselves out completely, accomplishing in a day what the rest of us have not.

As Flecha and Eisel climb off, the mechanics reach for their bikes. The rest of our bikes are lined up, looking new again, on a rack beside the truck. The mechanics ask if the bikes have worked properly, taking notes in a black book filled with requested adjustments. Each of us receives a new bike at the beginning of the season, and we constantly make minute adjustments to ensure they fit just right. We test different saddles, handlebars and stems until we find a combination that causes no discomfort. The bike should be an extension of the rider's body.

Riders become particular about their equipment in every way. For some, their choices are rooted in comfort. Others make changes to gain performance advantages, and a few respond to superstition. Having won, crashed or lost when using certain equipment, they keep it or discard it forever. Those who are especially particular, who have found a saddle that is comfortable or a shoe that is still snug after six hours of riding in extreme heat, will use non-sponsor-specific equipment, taping or painting over logos. Teams may also choose to do the same, if a sponsor's equipment isn't on a par with the rival teams'. Wheels will be built up without logos, and tyre labels will be inked over.

The mechanics begin washing off the spots of mud, streaks of sticky energy drink, spit and mucus from the handlebars, frames and wheels. They'll run through the gears and check the brakes and tyres to ensure everything is ready for the next training session. As they begin their routine, the riders nurse bottles filled with a liquid meal replacement to improve their recovery.

Having put on their sandals to protect the cleats on their cycling shoes from damage, Flecha and Eisel carry their shoes and helmets in one hand and their meal-replacement drinks in the other. In my first season as a professional, few of my teammates wore helmets out training. In many races, they weren't required. On the front of the peloton, we cruised along with the wind in our hair or with cotton caps perched high on our heads. Through the first years of my career a shift in rules and mentality began, as both the riders and the governing bodies became aware of the risk. In 2002, we could ride without helmets. In 2003, after Andrei Kivilev died during a race from head trauma sustained in a crash, the rules changed: helmets became mandatory, but they could be removed at the bottom of a mountain for the final ascent to the finish, as many riders complained the helmets were too hot to wear while climbing. The rule only caused chaos and the occasional crash, as the entire peloton pulled their helmets off, throwing them to soigneurs (assistants) at the roadside or having a domestique take eight helmets back to a team car. Before long the rule was scrapped and we had to wear helmets all the time. For the younger generation, who have worn them since they were kids, it is simply part of the uniform. They wear helmets every time they ride.

Although we move together, in pairs or pelotons at the training camps and races, we are also independent. Cycling is a team sport, but a solitary pursuit. We become introspective, analysing, calibrating and ingesting knowledge, thoughts and information to improve our performance. Although we rely on staff and teammates while racing, there is rarely anybody to wake us up in the morning while at home, to encourage us to ride, to ensure we do our training properly. Alone on a mountain in the pouring rain, we dig in and push on, alone. At the top, we reflect on the effort. We feel happy or disappointed. The sport requires commitment. We only switch off in the final thrusts of the racing season or in the off season, and even then it is a superficial and momentary lapse in the routine. Cycling tames its athletes. The ferocity of the individual can be seen on the bike, quelling tension, anger or demons of the past. Off the bike he is calm. The rage will not be seen in a bar fight. The emotion can be seen in a sprint, a pull on the front, or an attack.

We are all artists. On the bike we express emotion.

Brad greets each of us with a handshake. The massage therapist who has picked him up from the airport unloads a mountain of bags and a guitar. Brad has changed since we rode together in Girona just after Christmas. Like the rest of us, he looks leaner than he did just after the holiday feasting. His hairstyle changes by the month or by the race, and now it is long, hanging over his ears and his collar, like that of a character from the Muppets or a rock star. But underneath the mop of red hair is a skeletal face. During the last two seasons he has come to camp heavier. Now, even though it is early in the year, he looks ready to race and win.

Not only his physique has changed but his demeanour. He seems overly confident and aloof. Our conversation is all pleasantries, as it is when you haven't seen someone in a while. But even though we are teammates and friendly, he comes across as rudely arrogant and self-assured. He is not aware that he provokes this reaction. The rest of us wear our team clothing. He wears what he chooses. I know that his insecurities will remain starkly apparent until he feels comfortable in his environment. Within hours he will settle into the team, joking and keeping the riders at the dinner table laughing. But something more has changed in him. I can feel it as soon as he stands at the elevator and we chat. Brad derives his confidence from his performance on the bike. That means he must be riding well.

We offer to help with his bags, each of us pulling a case into the elevator. He has brought so many bags that he could be moving in for the duration of the spring. He has his guitar and his kettle. Whenever he can, he will escape from the bubble of the team to his room, which he will not have to share with a teammate. There he will find comfort. We all need a place that brings us back to reality. For him, it is with his music, his cup of tea and his family.

I've seen both sides of Brad, many times. When physically challenged he is unpredictable. He remains calm if he feels capable, can control the variables and knows he is good enough to win. To win, he needs a support team who know his mental and physical weaknesses, can call his bluff, and will be there to help him through dire moments. He needs someone to tell him when he is out of shape, when he isn't doing his job properly, isn't committed or is simply being an arrogant ass. Within Team Sky, he has now found a safety net he can rely on. Without that security and guidance, he falls to pieces. I saw that happen in 2010, before the Tour de France.

For three days, Steve Cummings, Brad and I were together with Sean Yates, our directeur sportif, Rod Ellingworth, our coach, a mechanic and a massage therapist to ride the key mountain stages of the 2010 Tour. As we had been in the Giro d'Italia, Steve and I were to be Brad's domestiques in the Tour. In the three-day camp, we would build on the working relationship we had developed during the first part of the season. In the Tour, Brad would rely on us to position him at the front of the peloton before all the crucial moments of the race. When he needed food or water, he would look to us. We would shelter him from the wind, stay with him when he had a flat tyre, guide him back to the peloton after his wheel was changed. To enable him to win or even finish in the top ten of the Tour, we had to be at his service every day until we could do no more. The more we rode together, the more we understood each other, how we moved on the bike, our weaknesses and strengths.

The three-day training camp in France was our final hard training session before the Tour. We would reconnoitre the routes while accumulating kilometres and testing our fitness in the mountains. It is a formula most teams use prior to the Tour, to prepare the riders and support staff for the three weeks they will have to endure. Riding the courses gives us reference points for the race.

Prior to the camp, we were naively confident in Brad's ability. In the Giro d'Italia, in May, he had held the leader's pink jersey after winning the opening prologue, had defended his top-ten position through the first week of hard racing in the wind and hills, and then had backed off as planned, to ride at an easier tempo through the final week. With two weeks of recovery training after the Giro he was supposed to have rebounded to become even stronger by July for the Tour. It was a formula that had worked for past Tour champions and one that had worked for him in 2009, when he finished fourth.

Our camp began in the Alps, where we rode three hard mountain finishes: one to Station des Rousses in the Jura mountains, another to Morzine-Avoriaz, and a tough day over the Col de la Madeleine to Saint-Jean-de-Maurienne. The stage to Morzine-Avoriaz was one I knew well. For three years, while I raced as an amateur in Annemasse, I had trained and raced on the routes the Tour would use. I had imagined one day racing over these roads in the Tour de France. My teammates in those days constantly referred to the feats of professionals as we passed the summits of climbs or rode through valleys. 'Piotr Ugrumov rode up here in the big chain ring,' we'd say, 'in 1996.' 'This is where Kelly descended in 1984 at 124 kph.' In our heads we became those riders as we accelerated over mountain tops and descended through switchbacks, leaning our bikes into the corners, the tyres squeaking every so slightly as they gripped the tarmac.

With Brad and Steve, I pictured myself again in the race, a mental game I've played since I was a boy. Our conversations, on the bikes and off, centred on the race, as we tried to prepare ourselves for what might occur. But we were deluded. Our mental images were off. And that slowly became clear during the camp.

As we climbed towards Avoriaz ski station, a steady climb with tight switchbacks and steep gradients that opens up to a straighter, gentler road near the summit, it was apparent Brad wasn't on form. Rain poured down, thunder clapped and lightning broke through the dark sky, and he seemed to give up. Perhaps it was the conditions. I felt good. My body seemed to move freely on the climbs, a sensation I hadn't felt in some time. The Giro had brought me up a level and had given me power I couldn't have attained through training alone. Steve seemed equally comfortable.

We glanced at each other as we tried to figure out what pace we should ride. We didn't want to drop Brad and demoralise him. We weren't riding hard; Brad shouldn't have been suffering. He should have been stronger than we were. But I also knew that Brad would mentally switch off when he wasn't motivated. Perhaps this was one of those moments. I hoped it was. Otherwise, he wouldn't be good enough to perform in the Tour.

But the following day on the Col de la Madeleine, where we were to do a race pace effort, it became clear that Brad didn't have the legs. Rod had mapped out our routes and our training programme. On the climb, we were to ride at the same speed as we would in the Tour. Steve and I were to set a tempo at the bottom, riding at a hard pace for as long as we could sustain it, with Brad tight in our slipstream. The moment our speed slowed, Brad was to push on to the summit, while Steve and I made our way up the mountain as best we could.

Riding to the mountain, we sat in behind the team car to simulate the speed of the peloton as it races towards a climb. At the foot of the climb, the car accelerated away and we were left to ride at our own speed. A kilometre into the twenty-eight-kilometre climb Brad was not behind us. He didn't say a word, he simply drifted away from our wheels. We slowed down until he was again in our slipstream and then resumed a slower tempo. Again, without looking back, I sensed he was no longer behind us. This continued for five kilometres. Eventually, Sean told us to ride at our own speed to the summit.

I rode up alone, ahead of the others, finding my rhythm, climbing into the mist and clouds. Few cars passed me. It was serene and quiet. In these moments, alone on a climb, my thoughts drift between the present – my effort, the numbers on my powermeter – to my past and my future. I rode hard, sweating and breathing heavily, because I wondered if I would ever get to race up the climb or even ride up it again. Sinking myself into the effort, I felt liberated. Nothing else mattered. Like so many times before, I wondered how much longer I would ride. This time, I wondered if I would be investigated for having doped in the past, as allegations had been made against me by an ex-US Postal teammate, Floyd Landis. If that happened, my career could end. I was living with guilt and shame; to keep on riding, to keep my job in the peloton, to avoid vilification, I reverted to secrets and lies. On the mountainside, climbing amidst the vibrant green grass, the mooing cows, the trickling streams, and the snow-capped peaks, I felt as if I could ride away from it and find solace away from my sins.

The team tried to believe Brad would be able to bounce back. Sean knew otherwise but he remained hopeful. He had ridden alongside Lance Armstrong as a teammate and had worked with him during his Tour de France victories. Today, Sean had seen Brad give up on the climb. On the phone after the camp he said, 'Brad sure ain't Lance,' or something like that. I agreed. But few people were like Lance. When pressed, Lance fought harder. He hated to lose, to be second-tier. He was the King; he was the best. Unlike Lance, I felt, Brad could take it or leave it. He didn't thrive on being at the top. In fact, he was least comfortable when in that spotlight. When he had our attention in the bus, he pretended he was somebody else, humouring us with an impersonation. To win, someone needed to guide Brad along the way, to keep him on track and stop him from hiding when he was ready to shine.

A rider who will win the Tour doesn't falter in the training camp only a few weeks prior to the start.

Roughly ten days before the Tour, Dave Brailsford, our manager, asked me how I thought Brad was riding. I told him that his performance at the camp was worrying but that he was a hard person to read, and that perhaps he would bounce back. He reassured me and himself that Brad had been tested on a thirty-minute hard climb in Girona, named Rocacorba, and had broken his previous record. Many of us had ridden that climb to test ourselves prior to major events. Brad had not only broken his record but the absolute record as well. The team's managers had invested too much in Brad to take another direction. Either they secretly knew he wouldn't perform, or they had talked themselves into believing he could.

Alone on the climb in Girona, without distraction or external pressure, he had soared uphill. His time was impressive, and it stunned the other professionals who had made the same climb in the past. But regardless of his impressive time in Girona, ten kilometres of solitary climbing was not the Tour.

In the Tour, despite Brad's best effort and the team's, we didn't achieve a single significant result. Midway through the race, when he was out of the top ten and knew he didn't have the legs to perform, he gave in. As the Tour progressed, he faltered physically. When he fell, he didn't bounce back up like a rider eager to regain the peloton, but lingered in the caravan, stopping and starting, as if he didn't want to be there at all. He was ready to pack up and leave, instead of setting a new finish line and battling on. His mental fragility and insecurity became apparent. He isolated himself in the back of the bus with his headphones on. His humour turned to unsavoury mockery. The team sank into a trough of negativity, one we would never climb out of. Not being in peak condition is one thing. Giving up because you're not meeting expectations is another.

To most of the riders and staff, it was a defeat that hurt. Brad was out of shape and the team was off the mark, but seeing him give in, without admitting it, was wrong. In a sport where we learn to fight until our bodies give in, it was a let-down to everybody who had devoted himself to the goal.

On the final stage, up the Champs-Elysées in Paris, our directeur asked Brad to lead out Edvald Boasson Hagen for the sprint finish. It was a small task – a few hundred metres of riding on the front of the peloton in the last kilometres of the Tour. The team was lined up to execute the plan, but in the final run-in, Brad wasn't there. He was in the middle of the bunch, alone, pedalling out the final metres in defeat. It was disappointing. Not because we lost, but because he wasn't there to give back to those who had helped him for three weeks. This was something I was unaccustomed to in a leader. Something fundamental needed to change in his attitude and in the way the team worked. But I also felt sad for him. The team had built up his ability, the media had broadcast it and the fans had idealised it. He was to be the first Brit to win the Tour. Yet, in the end, he didn't have the legs to fulfil their goals, their vision, their dreams, which must have put him in a lonely place. He was being paid to win races, and he wasn't completing the task. It is one thing to feel you've let down a team, but another to feel you've let down a nation.

When I arrived at the team bus he was already halfway through a can of beer with a second in his back pocket. I could feel his disappointment. And as he sat on the kerb outside the bus with his wife and children, signing autographs while sipping a Heineken tallboy, I had to wonder how much he wanted to be a star and how much he just wanted to be a bike racer. To win, he would need to learn to manage the pressure of leadership and, more importantly, the pressure of public expectations. Ultimately, it was naive and unfair to Brad to expect him to win in the Tour and lead a new team.

Throughout the race, Dave and his staff would sit in the back of the bus, trying to figure out how we could rectify the situation. They tried to come up with new tactical plans. They tried to animate Brad as he fell into a deeper funk. We were losing, and this was not something Dave was accustomed to after years of success and dozens of Olympic and World Championship medals earned while overseeing the British Cycling track squad. Fiercely competitive, he hated it. With a professional road team, there were more variables to control and more complexities, as there were more people to answer to and far more scrutiny from the sponsors and the public. On the track there were Olympic cycles, while with the road team there was a constant relentless pursuit of results.

Overall, the Tour and the season were a disappointment despite some consistent performances. Many teams might have been proud of our achievements, but for an outfit with a large budget and lofty goals, we had not won enough. There was no doubt that would change: nobody in management was happy with average results. The team had to be setting the standard, winning consistently, and winning the most important races.

Through the rest of the summer and the autumn, our managers reassessed their direction, the structure and the approach of the team. In a short period, changes occurred. The team roster was bolstered with talent, new doctors were hired, and incompetent or negative staff members were replaced. Brad was given ultimatums. He was expected to do his job properly, on and off the bike. Not only are we athletes but we are also ambassadors for companies. Our job is to ride fast and to interact with the public. Ultimately we are nothing more than rolling billboards. It was clear that Brad had neglected his obligations.

Now, in Majorca, as Jez and I walk towards the seaside on our usual evening stroll, I gaze into the hotel lobby's big windows. The glass reflects the sun as it begins to set in brilliant oranges and reds on the blue Mediterranean. In our reflection we do not look like two fathers in their late thirties. We look like two teenagers, bundled up in black branded clothing with black woolly hats pulled low. Through the glass, I can see riders huddled at the tables, coaches meeting over computers. We've seen this every day. Everyone seems calm and ready. Now, there are few variables the team can't control. Through experience our management and riders have quickly learned from their mistakes and have adapted. The team has evolved. Brad has changed. He is now watched closely. His training is monitored. To win the Tour he has become a disciple of the programme. With Sky, good riders can maximise their potential to become great.

The following morning we do a three-hour steady ride through the flat countryside. The group is large, since two waves of riders, one coming to the camp and the other leaving for home, have overlapped by a day. Mark Cavendish is there with his lead-out men and the Classics group. Brad is there with the climbers.

The air is damp and chilled, not yet warmed by the bright sun. We ride slowly along the coastal road and fall into formation, paired up in a long line hugging the right-hand kerb. The air becomes piercingly cold as we ride through the shadows of the empty resorts that tower over the coast. Of the fifteen or so riders, one or two slide to the back of the group to grab warmer clothing from the mechanic. He sits tucked into the back seat of the team car behind us in a nest of wheels, tools and clothing. Another rider drifts back to get his bike adjusted.

As we ride in a double file, each pair pulls off the front to share the workload with the others behind them. To peel off, the rider on the right moves right, the rider on the left moves left, reducing their speed gently to let the others pass. The two immediate followers slice between the pair and assume the lead, with the rest of the group following in their slipstream. The two who have just finished their turn on the front let the group glide past them until they can tuck themselves into the back and get out of the traffic as soon as they can. Together we are fluid and seamless.

Soon we leave the outskirts of the town and move into the countryside. The low winter sun is now on our backs. Our speed increases. We have found our tempo, one that is easy enough that we can chat to our partner yet fast enough to cover 110 kilometres in three hours.

At times our rhythm seems off. The riders who have completed their training week feel mildly fatigued from all the work we've done. Our legs ache slightly but are still powerful when pushed. The riders who have just arrived are eager to push the pace. Their legs and minds are fresh. They're like children ready to attack the ski slopes. But when the pace builds, a few riders complain, and the group slows slightly.

Brad assumes his position at the front and picks up the speed. He is wearing the jersey of the British National Champion, white with blue and red stripes across the chest, and is easily distinguishable from the rest of us in our blue, white and black uniforms. I sit directly in Brad's slipstream, behind his rear wheel, while Cav, my partner, is to my right, behind Alex Dowsett. Cav and I chat. Brad and Alex say very little. Alex initiates most of the conversation. The contrast between the two leaders is great, as is the tension. Although there is a remarkable potency within the group, it is apparent in our conversations that there is not room for two leaders. The races will decide who leads.

As the speed builds, the riders feel the increased pressure on their legs as they push to follow, and they begin moaning behind us. We speed into rural towns, with their ancient cream-coloured stone walls and mazes of narrow streets, but the tempo doesn't relent. The team moves quickly, skirting parked cars by inches and accelerating out of tight corners. Locals give a short cheer as we pass through town in a blur of colour. Our conversation, mixed with the ticking and whirling of the free-wheels and the squeal of the brakes, creates a symphony of noise against more routine small-town sounds: the rattle of bottles being delivered to a bar, the laughter of kids playing in a park, the clink of glasses on a terrace.

On a narrow farm road that cuts through an olive grove the group slows. We unclip and pull over to the side. Lined up like soldiers, we pee. During our brief stop riders gather around the team car, like seagulls at a picnic table, digging into the trunk for food, filling their pockets with energy bars. They grab cold water bottles from the cooler, replacing the empty bottles on their bikes. Some peel off layers of clothing, adjust their bikes with an Allen wrench or change wheels to test prototypes.

Climbing back on our bikes, we quickly resume our formation. Our pairs are reshuffled and now I am riding beside Brad instead of Cav.

As with most early-season conversations between professional cyclists, we discuss our race schedules for the coming months. Brad chimes off the races like a song he has memorised through repetition: Volta ao Algarve, Paris–Nice, Volta a Catalunya, Tour de Romandie, Critérium du Dauphiné, the Tour de France and the Olympics.

How will you approach them? Will you slowly build up towards the Tour? Or target another victory in the Dauphiné?

The goal is to win them all.

Every one of them?

Yes.

I nod. Okay. Inside I question whether he is being overly confident and too self-assured, or joking.

In the last twenty years, few cyclists have started the racing season with the goal to win from start to finish. It is unrealistic. The demands are too great and the chance of crashing, having a mechanical failure or falling ill is high.

But the team has a plan. Brad believes in it. They believe in him. And now he believes in himself.

4

Lying on the road, I could feel the tiny stones embedded in the smooth black tarmac. The thin layer of Lycra had been ripped from my torso, and I could feel the dusty surface of the road, warmed by the intense desert sun, against my skin, but I couldn't sense the burn of open wounds. That would come later. Adrenaline numbed the pain and kept my mind racing. Get up and go, is every rider's instinct. The peloton was speeding away from me, pushed by the tail-crosswind that had splintered it into echelons and created panic. I tried to get up from the road, but I couldn't move. Unable to raise my head, I stayed in a foetal position, trying to protect my body from other cyclists, motorcycles and cars. I saw the wheels speed past. Others stopped in front of me and behind. Soon, faces appeared. Some were familiar – my directeur sportif, Steven de Jongh, the mechanic Gary Blem, and Rod Ellingworth, who had been following in the team car. Others were strangers. I sensed no panic in their voices, which I would have heard if they'd thought I could get back into the race. These voices were calm. They'd seen my injuries, even if I couldn't feel them. Their voices made it clear that my body was beaten from the crash. They understood I wouldn't be riding to the finish. They told me not to move.

I closed my eyes as my mind raced. How badly was I hurt? When would I return to the peloton? A grey-bearded doctor hovered over me and asked simple questions: What was my name? What country was I in? His accent was strong, but I couldn't place it. Surely he was Belgian or French. I recognised him from the hotel elevator, where I had seen him that morning. I had nodded hello as I chatted with my teammates. Confident we would win, I had felt strong, healthy and ready to take on the race. Three hours later, in the middle of the Qatari desert, the same doctor now acknowledged my correct answer, and I felt relieved. At least I was lucid. Past crashes have made me fear the emptiness of a concussion. But now my head was intact, and I knew I could feel and move my toes and fingers. I would be okay.

From the corner of my eye, beyond my bent and broken bicycle, I could see movement. When a crash occurs, each directeur sportif stops to see if one of his riders has fallen. Cameramen stop, as well, to capture what might be the story of the race. The commissaires record the fallen rider's number. The race doctor surveys the damage. The ambulance waits, while a helicopter hovers overhead broadcasting the live images worldwide. Then the caravan of cars, motorcycles and vans behind the crash begins to move again.

Foreign hands cautiously lifted me onto the stretcher. Pain had begun to settle into my system. A brush of an elbow, a bump against the stretcher as they lifted it into the ambulance, the belt that strapped me down, all made me cringe. I became more aware of where I was hurt. Rod climbed into the back of the ambulance with the medic and sat precariously on a side-facing bench. The doors shut. We accelerated, and the stretcher shifted slightly. I bit my lip to ease the pain. Impatience unsettled me. I wanted this to be over with. I asked the medic to begin cleaning my wounds. He cut through my torn jersey to get to the grazes and cuts. They were superficial and secondary to my deeper injuries. In ten days my skin would heal. But I knew my arm was broken; lifting it even an inch seemed impossible. I feared my leg was also broken. Knowing my family had been watching the race on television in Girona and in Toronto, I asked Rod to call them to let them know I would be all right. He dialled and passed me the phone.

The moment I heard the concern in Dede's voice, I fought back tears. In that instant my mind moved away from the race to our home, our boys, the garden, the trampoline, football in the park, dinners on the patio. I didn't want to lose that for anything. Biting my lip and moving on, I told her to call my parents. They had emailed me just before we left the hotel to tell me they'd be watching the race. I assured her I was okay.

She asked again, 'Are you sure?'

'Yes,' I responded, unsure.

I had been in this position too many times before.

Our lives change with each crash, and all riders can remember the moment when a fall happens. Jez can recall the moment his collarbone broke in the Bay Series in Australia. Amidst the chaos of the crash, he says, the sound was as clear as a branch snapping in a quiet forest. I can remember with clarity the rider losing control of his bicycle that day in Qatar and falling in front of me. As the medic cleaned my skin, I closed my eyes momentarily. In that moment I could see it all happening again.

To a spectator, who sees so many crashes, our injuries may look no more serious than a splinter or a stubbed toe, nothing more than an irritation, quickly forgotten. But we feel our injuries with the same intensity as anyone else. They hurt. And our memories hold on to those life-changing moments. With each crash we slowly lose the fearlessness of a child. Caution, which blossoms with maturity, has lengthened my career but also may have cost me victories.

Cyclists accept grave injuries. Accustomed to breaking bones, patching wounds and watching our bodies heal, we become somewhat numb to the damage done. Fit and healthy, the cyclist's body recovers quickly. With a goal to get back on and ride, our healing is accelerated. Dwelling on the past, living with regrets and what ifs, only slows healing. But within ourselves, we are forever marked by a crash.

Few cyclists haven't known the moment before a fall. Every professional has experienced that moment repeatedly. We react and can only pray those reactions will keep us up or protect us. The moment never lasts more than a second. Our tyres failing to grip on a wet corner. Another rider wildly losing control. A car mirror hitting an elbow. Everything else that occurs afterwards becomes a blur. But those few split seconds will haunt a rider, making us question our movements on the bike forever afterward, as well as those of the peloton.

The vast majority of my teammates and peers have broken bones. Like our tan lines, our scars are part of our identity. Each scar has a story but the story is rarely recounted. Superstition seeps into our minds as we attempt to control our future. We will not speak of crashes in fear that the ominous moment will occur again. When the words are uttered we touch wood in an attempt to wipe away their consequences.

In the ambulance, Rod said, 'It was that bloody number 13 you've got on your back.' The luck of the draw. The race organisers had assigned number 13 to Barry. Not wanting to believe in superstition, I didn't flip the number upside down when I pinned it to my jersey, like so many others do in the hope that it will keep bad luck at bay. The signs were all there. In the morning, on the way to the race we had discussed crashes, medical protocol and hospitals, topics that riders usually avoid, especially on race day. Two years ago, when Rod had asked me what races I didn't want to start, I mentioned only one: the Tour of Qatar. I had ridden it before. If I rode it again, I felt the odds of crashing would increase. But I gave in, and decided to return. And now, in the ambulance, I thought about that decision. My mind shifted away from the thought and focused on the goal. Past crashes had taught me that a seemingly horrendous incident could, in the end, be for the best. Patience. Persistence.

Before the season began, I rode through the Majorcan countryside with my now retired contemporaries, Kurt Asle Arvesen and Bobby Julich. Both had become coaches with Team Sky. I asked them about retirement. It wasn't, Kurt said, his ageing body that spurred his decision to quit, but his fears. Accumulated crashes had made him apprehensive. He could recall the moment when the risk began to outweigh the reward. It was time to move on. Bobby spoke of a broken arm and, likewise, of the risk finally overshadowing the reward. Both talked about the changes to their lives now that they were retired. They seemed happy to be retired and said they didn't miss competing. I felt a twinge of jealousy.

Knowing my career was nearing its end, I wondered if this crash in the Qatari desert would be the one. I didn't want to believe it was. I had a season of racing left. I wanted to be back in the belly of the bunch, with the boys.

A cyclist can't predict the moment he will have had enough of the racer's life. We move from season to season, chasing childhood dreams and adult goals. Immaturity is fearless. With experience the cyclist's vision of his pursuit shifts until fear engenders hesitation when the time comes to squeeze through the gap.

Position determines who wins, loses or crashes. The odds of crashing, or being caught behind a crash, are greater at the back of the peloton. Over our race radios, we can hear urgency in the directeurs' voices when they tell us to move forward as we approach a dangerous section of a course. In that moment, dozens of directeurs each command their eight or nine riders to do the same thing: head to the front.

To win, the strongest teams now strangle the race, impose their tactics on the rest of the riders and try to control variables. The underdog has little chance. Despite increasingly challenging courses, pelotons often remain compact and massive until the final kilometres. Over the last fifteen years, the differences between riders' abilities have diminished because of better training, proper diets, a more international peloton and more aerodynamic, lighter equipment. The races have become more predictable. Often, only the injured or ill fall off the pace.

When nearly two hundred riders charge down a narrow, twisting, rural road three metres wide, crashes are inevitable. Cameras can't capture the chaos in the bunch. The peloton rarely relaxes. Within it, we ride inches apart, our elbows rubbing, our shoe buckles clipping sharp spokes, our tyres brushing up against each other's. There is precious little room to manoeuvre. Behind the first line of riders every inch of the road is used. To get to the front of the peloton, we accelerate up the dirt shoulder, a driveway, a sidewalk or a bike path while dodging spectators, parked cars, utility poles and potted plants. In our hasty dash to the front, we jump kerbs at 50 kph.

The constant live feed of news, which streams from a race over the internet and television, has increased the tension. A decade ago, seasons began progressively. The early races were often slower, and riders used them to gain fitness. Now, the first race of the season has become as important as the last. Training camps are held in December to ensure we'll be in top shape by the end of January. From the first race of the season in January until the last in October entire pelotons of 140 to 200 riders fight for attention. Often our employers consider us only as good as our last race. The battle is relentless.

Few races unfold without at least one crash. Often there's more than one, with ambulances carting the fallen to hospital. And then a rider dies. We accept his death as part of cycling. But is it? Perhaps the number of crashes could be reduced, injuries prevented and death avoided. But this will happen only if the riders, the organisers and the governing bodies take responsibility and promote change.

Here's one: courses should be designed to make races not only challenging but also safe. As automobile traffic has increased throughout the world, towns and cities have placed roundabouts, poles, speed bumps and islands in the roads to slow the cars. For the peloton, which often hurtles through towns at 50 kph or more, these obstacles need to be properly indicated or, better still, eliminated from the route.

As the ambulance passed the peloton, I caught a glimpse of the riders through the rear window. Not even fifteen minutes earlier, I had been riding with them. Now I felt as though my racer's identity had been stripped away. In twenty minutes they'd be finished. Immediately after crossing the line, they'd grab a drink from one of the team staff, hastily answer a few journalists' questions and gather around the team vehicles. They'd relive the race, discussing each significant moment in the final kilometres. They'd cuss like teenagers as they critiqued their rivals. In the ambulance, I already felt distant from their world. Only those in the peloton, who suffer together, can share those experiences. I knew I'd miss the camaraderie when I returned home.

5

The pain keeps me awake. The painkillers keep me from realising how awake. The sheets, my underwear and the gown are
damp with sweat. The room is dark. The blinds are up but the
greyness outside is only slightly brighter than the room, illuminated by red and green lights on the monitors. Rain taps against
the window. Manchester rain. The odour of the room is now my
odour and smells natural to me. I am sure it is the scent of dead
skin, sweat and antiseptic. I've stepped into the rooms of enough
wounded teammates to recognise the aroma.

Only thirty hours ago I was racing in the Middle East. Bad
experiences in prior seasons had taught the head team doctor to
ship me out of Qatar on the earliest flight for the UK so I could
be re-examined and operated on by a surgeon they knew would
do the job well.

The Qatari emergency room had been crowded with injured
immigrant construction workers. I left there with a CD of my
X-rays and my arm in a plaster cast. Rod drove me in the team
car back to the hotel. He took care of me like I was a brother,
which comforted me more than he realised. The team doctor
had left me with Rod, to take care of other concerns or just to
get some sleep. He couldn't understand why the team was flying
me home instead of leaving me in Doha to have surgery. He
was like many other team doctors. As long as I was in a hospital
somewhere, anywhere, he didn't question the outcome. Fortu-
nately, this team was built on different principles.

Cycling teams cannot afford to slow their pace. To them, an

injured rider becomes a liability within a structure that is based on year-to-year sponsorship contracts. To sustain themselves financially, they push on and forget about the fallen. It was a reality I knew and accepted. The injured became an afterthought, mentioned every now and then at mealtimes when other riders asked how he was doing. For the most part, they were left to heal alone at home, with little help from the team. Most teams would have left me in the Qatari hospital, alone, as the race rolled on. But not Sky.

I'd been given morphine in the ER. It flowed through my body, soothing the pain, but also making me feel dizzy and nauseated to the point where I felt delirious and slightly paranoid. I hadn't eaten since midway through the race. Hours had passed. I asked the team doctor for a Coke or some food, anything to lift my blood sugar. He shrugged. There was nothing available, he said, although he didn't put much effort into the search. When Rod arrived and saw my condition, he was furious at the doctor. He stormed off to search for food, came back with a drink and said food was on the way. Shortly after this race, the team fired the doctor. He had spent too long in cycling and had become far more concerned with our performance and his image than our health.

Back in my room at the hotel, the race medical staff patched me up. It was well past midnight. Jez was in a bed beside me, watching and cringing as they scrubbed, wiped and stuck bandages on. Our team doctor wouldn't do the job, for reasons he never explained. I wasn't disappointed. I doubt if he'd have done the job well anyway. My cyclist's hunger had set in again and I had become hypoglycaemic. My body raced to recover from my effort on the bike and my injuries from the crash. Between applications of each bandage, I devoured dinner. A nurse scrubbed the sand and grit from my weeping wounds with a plastic brush. With a mouth full of food, I winced.

Later, I woke up in the middle of the night to pee, but I couldn't put any weight on my leg to walk to the bathroom. Moving slowly from my sweat-soaked sheets, I reached for the wooden suit rack near the bed and used it as a crutch to inch my way across the room. Jez woke up and asked if I was okay. Not wanting to disturb him further, I lied, said yes, so he would get his sleep before the race. But, instead of peeing, I felt like throwing up from the pain. It was then I knew my leg was fractured. The doctors hadn't identified the injury.

Although my gut told me something wasn't right with my leg, I tried to believe it was all right. Cyclists often overlook their own injuries. Either our pain thresholds are too high, medical advice is poor or we pretend the injuries don't exist.

Back in England, the surgeon catches what the doctors in Qatar missed. Before he operates on my arm, he spots a small crack in my femur. He gives me a crutch so that I can keep my weight off my leg. With a broken arm, that will be tough. He advises me to stay off the leg for six weeks. That will be even tougher.

In Spain, my wife's mind is at ease knowing I'm a short plane trip away in Manchester. If there are complications, she can reach me quickly.

Here, in a clean private hospital, I am fed with medicine. It drips slowly into my arm. The drugs are unknown to me, and I don't ask what they are. Under other circumstances, I would ask to ensure I didn't ingest a substance banned in cycling. But the pain is too intense for me to care. Racing is distant. Everything seems distant. A glossy cycling magazine, brought to the hospital by one of the team staff, remains unopened beside my bed.

Once again I hate cycling. I turn slightly, and the pain intensifies, then abates. I lift my recently repaired arm. It is numb, a dead weight that the rest of my body has just enough force to move.

An empty tea cup and two open and empty plastic HobNob packets clutter the bedside table. My phone sits in the midst of the mess. I poke at it to wake it up to see the time: on the screensaver is a photo of my children with '4:30 am' across the image. The phone has buzzed all night as messages arrived from North America. I read them but can't remember what they say. The wounds, the fractures and the drugs are turning my consciousness patchy and incoherent. The morphine is killing time. I'm in and out of consciousness, but the ache never subsides. Someone has told me that bone pain is the worst kind. I hope there is nothing worse. The relentless ache creates sleepless nights, blurs my focus and produces angst and irritability. But like the pain of riding a bike as fast as possible up a mountain, I've suppressed the memory. Only when I relive those days do I recall how horrible that pain can be. Suppression is how humans cope. And persist.

Unable to find comfort I press the call button. And wait. Chirpy in the middle of the night, the nurse arrives. She pokes at my arm, checking the IV port and looking at the lines and bags that feed the drugs. Since my first season racing as a professional in Europe I've slowly become accustomed to needles and medicine. But I remain uncomfortable.

As a boy everything medical made me uneasy. At check-ups I touched only what I had to in the paediatrician's office. I stayed awake at night if I knew I would be getting a shot in the arm the next day. I ignored Tommy Simpson's biography, which stood on my father's bookshelf, because I was frightened by the cover image of Tommy with pills and syringes. My father became emotional when I asked about Simpson and his overdose in the 1967 Tour de France, on the Ventoux. When telling the story, my dad spoke as if he had lost a friend. After hearing the story of the life the drugs had taken, I didn't dare touch the book. Years later, when I told Lance Armstrong about my fear of the book while at a training camp in California, he chuckled.

Simpson was one of my father's heroes. A Londoner, my father had followed his career in 'the Comic', the cyclist's nickname for *Cycling Weekly*, a magazine that he continues to read after sixty years. Simpson was one of the few British riders who had succeeded at the top level on the continent. To most British cyclists, the cultural divide was far greater than the short physical distance across the channel. Or perhaps they returned home prematurely because the continent was so close. For a North American, or an Australian, the distance made the sacrifice greater, intensifying the pressure to succeed. We had a harder time returning home.

Pushed to our limits, our perspectives shift. In the rooms next to me, I'm sure there are people thinking similar thoughts whether they've just had breast implants or they're being treated for pneumonia. Hospitals, injury, illness, pain, and recovery put everything into question. In bed, there is nothing to do but think. In hospital beds I often question everything I've done with and in my life, and I wonder about the direction I will take next.

The nurse leaves and returns with another two bags of medicine. She replaces the empties and continues with her routine check: pulse, blood pressure, temperature, and oxygen saturation.

Anything else I can get you?

Another pot of tea and a few more biscuits, please.

I've had three cups of tea since the surgery. It seems to be the only thing that truly comforts me.

Earlier, after the surgery, I awoke in a trance from the anaesthetic. Time was lost somewhere. Hours seemed like minutes. The surgeon's name was Adam. He asked me how I was feeling. I vaguely remember him saying the surgery had gone well and that, despite the flesh wounds – what cyclists call road rash – he and his colleagues had fastened a plate to the bone. I shouldn't worry about infection, he said. But now my recollection of our conversation remains sketchy. Soon afterwards, I remember that a nurse came by and asked if I would like anything. That was six hours ago.

Despite numerous broken bones, I have never been confined to a wheelchair or crutches. The thought of sitting still, idle, for six weeks scares me more than the damage. A fractured femur will take that long to heal, I've been told. I must rest, although I had to bargain with the doctor for a shorter sentence.

I haven't been off a bike for more than a few weeks since I was two years old. Even when I broke my back and had to wear a corset, I rode the indoor bicycle. I rode in a doorway so that I could raise my arms and hold onto the top of the door frame while I pedalled to keep my back straight and pressure off the broken vertebrae. I rode that way for an hour a day, every day, for a month. That crash had scarred me as much mentally as it had physically. Riding helped me understand the trauma. Just turning my legs in circles was therapy for my mind. As much as the bike had hurt me in the crash, it calmed me and helped me heal in my recovery.

What can I do to keep sane if I'm confined to a bed, a couch or a wheelchair? Time will tell. The hospital bed is not the place to worry about such things. I sip my tea. It eases the pain.

The flavour, as it always does, brings me back to my parents' bedroom in Toronto. Each morning, when I was a small boy, I would climb into their bed, lying under the warmth of the duvet, tucked tightly between their bodies while they listened to the radio and read the newspapers. We all sipped tea and dunked biscuits. There was no better place to be. Snow accumulated on the windowsill. The morning sun shone through patterns etched by ice crystals on the glass, and I imagined mystical places and wonderful objects. But, with time, experience has tainted those wondrous images in a boy's mind.

In the hospital bed, with tea in hand, I gaze through the window, beyond the raindrops on the glass and into the darkness of the Manchester morning. I sink deeper into the bed and try not to think of what I have lost. Despite the pain, I tell myself, good will come of it.

6

Days before I crashed, Jez and I had been comparing our physiques in the hotel room, flexing our legs in the mirror and pinching our bellies to gauge the fat. Every rider does it, even at thirty-eight years old. Our weight is a sign of the work we've done, or the work that needs to be done. Like ballerinas or boxers, we are weight-obsessed. Our power-to-weight ratio determines our performance and, in the mountains, who wins. To ensure we are on track to perform, our coaches, doctors and physiotherapists monitor us closely.

While away at races, just after we wake up we are summoned to the doctor's room, where our weight and urine are checked to ensure we aren't dehydrated. After the race, we strip down and are weighed again to see how much fluid we've lost. The grams of water we've lost should be replaced by the following morning. Dehydrated, we can no longer perform.

In the team bus, riders comment on each other's vascular legs and muscle definition. Being lean is usually a sign of fitness, or form, or drug use. On the start line, we judge our rivals by their weight. We know that a chubby rider will struggle and that a lean rider is one to watch. But in comparison to the spectators who line the road, even the heaviest riders are thin.

Since I was a teenager, when Mirek Mazur, my Canadian provincial team coach, first advised me on how a cyclist should eat, I have been aware of my weight. At times, my weight consumed me and affected me.

Sky's team nutritionist, Nigel, schedules us for check-ups at each camp, and often visits the races. With calipers, he pinches our skin at several places to calculate body fat. He checks our weight on a digital scale, notes it and graphs it. If we are overweight, he suggests that we diet. Every gram is counted. Rarely are we considered too thin.

During the camp in Majorca, Jez had his fat checked by Nigel. He was heavier, fatter, than he had hoped. With his knee injury, he was gaining weight as he was training less. He was anxious. We had all felt the same anxiety. Nigel advised Jez on what to cut off his diet to lose the kilograms quickly.

Each evening before dinner, after we had our massages, we went out along the boardwalk. It was our brief escape from the training camp environment, where everyone seems singularly focused. The environment wasn't stifling, but it seemed oddly false. We lived in a bubble, away from the world, where real things were going on and people had real problems. Within the camp environment we could be productive, train properly and consistently and focus solely on one objective. But after two weeks it began to feel unhealthy.

Walking along the sea front, as the setting sun reflected on the water in brilliant orange and red tones, I imagined strolling with my wife and children and watching them play in the sand. I'm sure Jez was thinking the same.

Moving incessantly, I often want to be where I am not. The life of the racing cyclist is lonely. I am rarely home long enough to fall into my family's rhythm, and I feel unsettled everywhere. As infants, our children were unaccustomed to my presence at home and wanted their mommy when they were hurt or tired. Each time I came home, I disrupted their routine and their pace. After a few days I would settle in, then leave again for another camp or race. At the races, I am with my teammates twenty-four hours a day. We share rooms, eat together, race together and travel together. There are few solitary moments. The relationships seem as close as a family, but that's an illusion. Ultimately, we are just business associates. Each season we become close to one or two teammates. In Jez, I have found a friend with whom I can share my deepest fears, greatest joys and darkest moments.

On a bench by the sea front, a group of teenage and twentysomething boys, who were likely the same age as many of our teammates, sat uncomfortably. They wore tight jeans and had pulled their hoods over their heads to shield themselves from the cold air or to hide their faces. They sipped from large litre bottles of Xibeca beer and took drags from their rolled-up cigarettes. One of them dragged hard on a joint and passed it along. This seemed to be their evening routine. We'd seen them each evening while we walked. A girlfriend hovered around the group, bouncing occasionally to a beat playing on her mobile phone, then dived in for a drag and a slug.

We walked slowly, shuffling along the tile boardwalk. We could feel the day's efforts on the bike in each step. Like sore teeth my quadriceps ached. With movement they pulsed as if blood was surging towards the damaged muscle to heal it. My calf muscles ached each time I stepped up a kerb. The joints in my knees were tender. The tendons, unaccustomed to the intensity of the hard intervals, ached from being worked to their limit. In a week, they would adapt to the pressures. Cyclists hate walking. During the racing season we aren't comfortable doing much other than pedalling. We even turn away from the other sports we love. Regardless of their fitness, those who are forced into other forms of exercise because of the weather struggle with the transition back to cycling.

The seaside resort town was deserted. Most shops were shuttered for the winter. The shops that were open were empty. In the cafe, our destination, the waiter was deep in conversation with a friend when we arrived. There were no other customers. The beaches, void of tourists, were serene.

In the cafe, Jez and I talked about cycling. We couldn't leave it in the hotel. The team dynamic had changed with the influx of new riders, who came with Cav or were hired to help Wiggo in the mountains. The team had been loaded up with proven talent. We should win consistently. We should dominate the stage races and the Classics alike. But the tension within the group was unsettling the ambiance, so there were no longer any guarantees that the team would become a dynasty which could win consistently over several seasons. Jez and I could feel it. And we chatted about it.

Jez sipped on a hot chocolate, breaking his diet. I drank tea and we munched on a shared plate of cookies. Even though I had burnt through thousands of calories while training, the cookies seemed like a treat at the end of the day. Eating them made me feel guilty. For years, my coaches, directeurs and nutritionists have urged me not to eat them. Jez felt the same way. Even in old age, our guilt was hard to ignore.

When I was an amateur, I rode for a team in Annemasse, France. Everybody associated with the team or even interested in cycling would comment on my weight. When I was thin, I would hear *Il est en forme*. When I was heavier, they'd pinch my waist or cheek and ask, *T'es un peux gros, non?* Like models or cattle, our value seemed based on our weight.

Teammates became bulimic, purging themselves if they ate too much, for fear they wouldn't perform. Others binged and then starved themselves in guilt, or rode for hours more than their training regimen required to burn the extra fuel. One of my amateur teammates ate desserts with the back of his spoon, to make them last longer, and to avoid overeating. Others chewed sweets and spat them out; they craved the flavour but feared the calories.

I considered the value in everything I ate: Was it worth eating? How would it affect my performance? Would I gain weight if it was too rich or too sweet? Would I bloat from the salt? I weighed myself several times a day, became depressed when my weight went up, content and confident when it went down. I no longer enjoyed meals as I once had, because there was always the sense of craving, pleasure and then guilt. During races or at training camps, coaches criticised our choices at meals, even though we were burning thousands of calories a day. At training camps and races when I was an amateur, the staff searched our rooms for hidden food like mothers looking for Hallowe'en candy stashed under a bed. I was encouraged by coaches to cut out fat, dairy, or some other food in order to follow whatever diet was the trend of the moment.

A teammate in Annemasse binged on chocolate spread, spooning it out of the jar when his father, a retired professional, was out of the kitchen. Once caught in his indiscretion, he was berated by his father for overeating and for not doing *le métier*, his job. Eating properly, like training for several hours a day and sleeping at least eight hours a night, was an integral part of the job. Bicycle racing was not a sport but a way of life: a job, a hobby and a passion wrapped into one. Despite the sacrifice, it was a life I wanted and one I thought family and friends expected me to pursue, even from a young age. Those expectations were what I perceived, but now, looking back, I see they were solely my own. It was the identity I created through my passion and my dreams, and those who cared for me never pressured me to assume those expectations. I did that all on my own.

With time I understood that I needed to find balance to be happy. Although I still consider every bite, since weight remains a factor in performance, I no longer measure and obsess. Extreme diets did more damage, both mentally and physically, than they were worth. Being a father, ageing and dealing with injuries, has forced me to balance my priorities.

Yet the sport allows only a minimal degree of balance. Cyclists reach for extremes in search of even the smallest gain. With each 0.5 per cent gained, the cyclist hopes the suffering will diminish and results will improve. The optimum is intangible. The pursuit of it consumes us. Cycling never gets easier; the rider's place within the peloton shifts. Even the very best lose far more than they win. There are always more races to win, mountains to climb, speeds to exceed and goals to set. As I matured and learned through experience, it became clear to me what I could and could not do. At thirty-four, I felt I had found my place in the peloton. No longer pushing to achieve what I wasn't physically or mentally capable of, I found solace in doing what I could do well.

Insecurity haunts the cyclist. It festers into jealousy and creates divisions within a team. Unsure of their place in the group and unhappy with their abilities, insecure cyclists often end up as misfits, outsiders. Cycling teams can accommodate several roles and personalities, but individuals who never feel comfortable with their place in the structure alienate themselves. Competition within a team can be healthy. It can inspire the entire team to a higher level. But when too many riders are vying for leadership, infighting and other problems develop.

Finishing our walk, Jez and I arrived back at the hotel. The mechanics were still working on the bikes, hosing them down, adjusting them, and building and rebuilding. When they aren't following the training rides in the team car, mechanics are working on the bikes. They're up before we wake, and they're still at it after we've gone to bed. They feel the pressure of performance and accountability for failures. Our safety depends on their work: an over-tightened titanium bolt will snap; a poorly glued tubular tyre will roll off the rim. They have to be meticulous in everything they do. I imagine they anxiously run through mental checklists as they lie in bed at night.

In the hotel lobby, riders played chess, others shot pool, paged through tabloid magazines, or lounged with their legs up, chatting with journalists, teammates or staff. In the corners of the room, some riders sat with their coaches, staring at a computer screen, poking at data on spreadsheets and graphs, planning for the season, or analysing the day's training. Empty coffee cups were scattered throughout the lounge.

Bags of clean laundry, washed after the training ride by the massage therapists, sat in a pile at the entrance to the dining room for us to take to our rooms after we finished our meal. We are catered to on every level.

Like hungry dogs waiting to be fed by their owner, the riders milled around the entrance to the dining room until it opened. The cyclist's appetite is insatiable after a long intense day on the bike. Seconds after the food was placed on the buffet the riders hover around like bees on honey. Few cyclists eat slowly; they race to satiate their hunger. Every meal counts and none is missed. That doesn't mean we aren't cautious about what we consume. Fatty meats, fried food and cakes are all passed over for fish, lean beef, rice, vegetables and fruit. The team staff dig into the food we avoid.

After dinner the riders gathered in the hotel lobby and bar and resumed their earlier positions. Some sat off in corners, speaking on the phone. In shared rooms, I've heard my teammates speak with their spouses, girlfriends and children. The tone of their voice becomes softer, quieter and more endearing, or sometimes tense as they try to resolve domestic issues and disputes. With our mobile phones, email and social media we are constantly connected, yet there is still emptiness and a longing that we cannot satisfy without human touch. The distance is a haunting void.

Late at night, after we put down our books, turned off our phones and shut down our laptops, Jez and I lay awake in the darkness chatting. A shaft of light from the boardwalk pierced through a gap in the drapes, illuminating a white line across the black ceiling. We chatted about cycling. About riders. About building a team, creating our fantasy team. We brought up riders' names, listing their strengths, weaknesses and what they would contribute to our squad. We thought back to races where we had been impressed by a performance unseen by the television audience and by the directeurs who followed behind, but which was felt by the peloton. A performance that made our legs hurt. Our fantasy team was made up of unknown riders who, with the right guidance and environment, had the potential to become champions or selfless domestiques.

Our dream team was stacked with riders who have qualities that can't always be seen from the sidelines. Their qualities are felt when they accelerate, seen in the way they pedal or overheard in conversations with their rivals and teammates.

We were riding for one of the best teams ever assembled, yet we were still building a dream team based on what we had learned in our careers. Bike wheels never stop spinning.

7

I knew the muscles I had built and trained through the winter would melt away as my broken bones healed. What takes months to build will be lost in weeks when you are idle. My fitness would be worse than it was when I had resumed training in November, after my off-season break. What I didn't know was how much more I would lose in the six weeks that I would be immobile with the broken leg.

Now my thoughts shifted to the rest of my career. Would the injuries be the end of it, or would I return to a decent level? Ending like this was something I couldn't handle. Falls had distanced me from my chosen career; fear, which was absent in my youth, created apprehension. But I wanted to retire at a peak, feeling light on the bike, racing on a course that suited me. I had thought that retiring in Montreal, at the one-day World Tour race, would be ideal. Now, broken, I couldn't think about riding, but I couldn't think about stopping either. Floating in a world created by pain, anger, frustration and painkillers, I went between hating cycling and loving it. Perhaps I felt a fear of loss, as well.

Before the crash, I had only just had the opportunity to use the fitness I developed over the winter. The Tour of Qatar was meant to be a lead-up race to the Classics, the prestigious and tough early-season one-day races in northern Europe, where we could continue to build fitness, rediscover the rhythm of the race, and refine the way we rode together and executed our race tactics. This year, the team's third, was different from the first two. Like the dominant teams of past generations, Sky was now setting a standard that others tried to match. With a significant budget and management with a vision, the team was able to do what others were not: they not only hired top riders with proven results but were also able to nurture talent to produce champions. This is what Dave Brailsford had promised.

At our first training camp in 2010, just outside Valencia, Dave B had explained the team's policy and how the trainers, mechanics, soigneurs, directeurs and doctors would be involved with our care. We were a drug-free team, yet they would do everything within the legal limits to improve our performance. The riders listened and agreed. At the training camp, we were told the goal was to be not only the best cycling team in the world, but the best sporting team. The ideal seemed lofty, but we were eager, competitive, confident, and knew the clout and budget Sky has, and the dominance British Cycling had achieved on the velodrome.

In the team's first year, Chris Froome was a below-average domestique as he struggled with illness and injury and was unable to achieve any significant results. His performance was subpar, to the point where he wondered whether or not his contract would be renewed. Physically he was gifted, but he needed proper guidance and training. Riders who are willing to adapt and learn will succeed. All it takes is a bit of guidance that instils confidence. In a few months, Froome went from being a rider who worried about his contract to a Grand Tour contender, after he finished second in the 2011 Vuelta a España.

Sky had the team it needed to win Grand Tours, Classics and sprints. As long as they created and maintained an atmosphere in which riders were committed to the team effort, and as long as they managed the riders' personalities so they would work together, the team would succeed.

With the best sprinter in the world, Mark Cavendish, the team had the opportunity to win with consistency, if we could control the race tactics and execute our plans. For Cav to dominate as he had in past seasons, it was crucial we refine our ability to work together to put him in position to win. Without the help of teammates in a finale, a good sprinter can win on occasion, but with the aid of teammates he can win with consistency.

In the first days of the Tour of Qatar, just before I crashed, we had struggled to find the balance where every rider on the team knows his role, is in the right place at the right time, and carries out his duties. Davide Appollonio, a young Italian sprinter with the physical ability to do the job, didn't have the confidence or experience to position Cav for the final charge to the finish line. And Cav didn't trust him; he could tell Davide couldn't do it. The line-up was shifted, and Cav won. But something was still missing. Things weren't going as smoothly as they had in the past. Cav was accustomed to a team that rode in synch, but our balance was off. There were too many ideas of how we should adapt to win. Our fitness was good enough, but without camaraderie, understanding and selflessness, we would not achieve our goals. With the media spotlight on the team, we were expected to win. We tried to force something that should have been innate, but the personalities didn't click.

Early in the 2012 season, at the training camp, it was clear there was tension between the three team leaders, Cav, Chris Froome and Brad. The rivalry between the British cycling stars was not unexpected. Chris and Brad had finished second and third in the 2011 Vuelta a España, a race they would have won had they had confidence in their combined strength during its first week, and Cav was the best sprinter in the peloton. There was jealousy, as well, within the hierarchy. Each leader felt he had to prove his worth to win over his teammates.

After subpar results in 2010 and good ones in 2011, Dave Brailsford hired Cavendish to guarantee results in 2012 that would position us as the best team. There was hope that Cav would alleviate some of the pressure on Brad, and relieve him of the role of leader which didn't come naturally to him. Cav is the dominant sprinter of his generation and arguably the best ever. Since the age of twenty-two he has consistently won more races than almost any other professional. A sprinter who can win throughout an entire season will keep a team buoyant. Before Cav, Sky was missing a true leader and someone who could win with consistency.

In 2007, 2008 and 2009, I rode with Cav on HTC-Columbia, the dominant team of the period. Cav's victories made all of our jobs easier. They gave us confidence in our ability to control the race. More importantly, with each victory the pressure changed. Like an avalanche gaining momentum as it thunders down a mountain, we felt as though we were unstoppable. Winning became easier as other teams, naively, let us dictate the pace and were happy to follow in our slipstream while we grew stronger and more confident. By signing Cav, now the World Champion, Sky's management hoped the same thing would occur in 2012. At the first training camps, the team assumed a confidence that bordered on arrogance.

In Qatar I was just beginning to rediscover the rhythm of racing. The first races of the year are a shock to the body. At home or even in training camp, it is difficult to mimic the conditions of racing. In the slipstream of a motorbike we can simulate the accelerations and the speed of a race, but still we control the effort. In races, we can't control the unpredictable external pressures – the peloton, nervousness, our rivals, the wind – and they force our bodies and minds to adapt.

Jez had been my roommate through the training camps in Majorca. With him, I was comfortable. We could empathise and sympathise with each other's problems, as parents, husbands, and veteran cyclists. Similar life-changing experiences and a shared passion for cycling were the foundation of our friendship. There were few others with whom we could speak honestly about those experiences and emotions. As we neared retirement our friendship grew stronger.

With each season the generation gap between the younger riders and the veterans felt exponentially greater. Laid out on their beds, they punched at keyboards for hours, playing games and keeping their social network alive. Or, with headphones blocking out their surroundings, they immersed themselves in films. They seemed more self-assured and self-focused, the result of egos fed by social media and a constant stream of race results and live feeds over the internet that placed value on performances that would have gone unnoticed in earlier times. Every rider is a hero in his own world, but before we became connected to the outside world by phones and the internet, our focus was on the team.

Now, after the races, our phones ring on the bus, and we each report our version of events to our friends, family, followers and reporters. The change has occurred during my career. In the mid-1990s, when I was an amateur, few riders had mobile phones. Those who had them would call home after races, often standing in a field, like cattle looking for a good patch of grass, away from trees and buildings, where they could find a clear signal. Riders then began carrying computers, asking each other for the local access numbers so they could send emails and race reports home. The laptop was a wonderful way to stay connected. It made our lives easier and gave us comfort in tougher moments. But perhaps we have become too connected. There's less sense of community in the peloton and less solidarity amongst teammates and riders. Self-aware narcissism is the unhealthy side effect. The connectedness of the digital world has made us less connected with those around us in the present. We are no longer absorbed in the moment or immersed in our environment. Our digital tentacles reach far beyond the actual community. A teammate once noted that many riders, especially the Americans, seemed more concerned with getting online to report on a race than with racing well.

At home with broken bones, I was reconnected with my family. But this time I couldn't train, travel or walk. I was with them day and night, for months, something I hadn't done since our boys were born. Nor had I spent this much time at home with Dede since our marriage. Being home, in one place, without a training programme to follow, was something I had rarely experienced since adolescence. I realised how much I had missed while I had been away. I also started to feel like a dad.

8

The spring air already held the humidity of the coming summer. Lawns were a lush green, full of moisture, yet to be bleached by the hot summer sun. The trees formed a canopy over the neighbourhood streets as I raced home from high school. My shirt was untucked, my blazer unbuttoned and fluttering in the wind, my tie loose and my wool pant legs held tight with rubber bands. At the house, I plunked my rusty old mustard-yellow mountain bike down in the backyard, opened the back door, drank a glass of cold orange juice and raced up to my room to exchange my sweaty school uniform for cycling clothing. It was ten minutes to four. In forty minutes I would meet a group of friends to ride, our daily routine since the snow melted in early March.

Clothed in the club's colours, a blue-and-white jersey with black shorts, I ate a snack at the dining-room table, and then put my head down for ten minutes, closing my eyes, to catch up on the sleep I had lost to meet a deadline or finish home-work when I'd been out riding until dusk. The few moments of rejuvenation were interrupted by a knock, then the creak of the opening door, followed by the familiar hello of a friend, Paul, who was already opening the fridge to pour a glass of juice and digging into the cookie jar when I arrived in the kitchen. His face was flushed from riding, sweat matting his hair and making his arms glisten. He was also dressed in blue and white with black shorts. We were not only a cycling team but something more, a tribe perhaps. Our bond went beyond the sport. We were teenagers, maturing through our experiences and discoveries, which would form our characters and make us unique in a city of millions where few rode bikes.

Sitting on the back porch, Paul ate and drank, while I pumped up the tyres on my racing bike, the latex tubes having lost air overnight. Another two riders arrived, Mike and Glenn, both our age, fifteen, and dressed the same. They hoovered a few cookies and slugged down a drink. We went to different schools and lived in different neighbourhoods. Riding brought us together. Each rider had a unique bike. Some were a mismatch of parts and colours, cobbled together over years, as components failed and were replaced or as parents presented gifts. Our bikes somehow told a little story about our lives at home and perhaps even our personalities. The way they were cleaned, the choice of parts, the colour, the position and the brand reflected the lives we lived. Functionality trumped elegance in every machine.

Riding down our cobbled drive, the bikes clattered as they bounced and as we fumbled to slide our leather shoes into the toe-clipped pedals. Out on the street we tightened the straps before we began our journey north. As we passed an office building with mirrored windows we each gazed at our positions as we tried to emulate the pros in the way they sat on their bikes, held their handlebars and perched their cycling caps high on their heads with the peak low over their brows.

In half an hour we would be in the sprawling suburbs and in forty-five minutes the open farm fields, with ominous signs posted in the fields of corn advertising future neighbourhoods. With each passing racing season we could see the city encroaching on the countryside, on our training grounds, where we would escape for the evening and ride in reverie.

The racing season was already well under way. We had ridden its opening races under falling snow. The cold air bit into our lungs with the first hard effort of the year, our movement restricted by the layers of clothing, the thick gloves, the hats under our helmets and the tights on our legs. I still didn't feel like a racing cyclist but a tourist. I felt heavy and clumsy on my bike from an off season of hockey and cross-country skiing. As the winter faded and grass patches became apparent on the once snow-covered lawns, we rode farther. Slowly we evolved into racers, moving from our fixed-wheeled winter bikes to our race bikes, cautious not to ride too big a gear and damage our still underdeveloped muscles and tendons.

Through the spring, summer and autumn, we raced most weekends, sometimes driving south to upstate New York, Michigan or Ohio or east to Quebec. These were life-changing experiences for boys, some who had never been out of the country, province or city. When there wasn't a scheduled race we would ride our own races, which were nothing more than long training sessions in the country, to places we had never been before, the four or five or eight of us racing each other as if we were in a foreign land. In our heads we could hear the screams of the spectators as we raced down empty country roads with nothing but the occasional tractor working a field. The bike made us feel empowered. We were free to go wherever we wished. It also gave us a goal, something to do after school, and a camaraderie unlike any other. For a few hours, we could run away, forgetting about homework, exams, deadlines and social teen awkwardness, to a spiritual space in our otherwise normal lives, a space we didn't yet know would forever mark us.

With each ride it felt as if we were reaching for something new. Our friendships grew. Our fitness improved. We went farther and came home with stories of moments that became the memories I now cherish. I think back on those moments more often than I would ever have predicted. The trophies I won then and over a lifetime now sit in boxes in the basement or on a shelf in my dad's bike shop, or else they are long gone, having been put on the kerb with a box of old T-shirts when, at some point, they became clutter. But the memories, like the moments, remain pure.

Decades later, when I am back in Toronto, I again ride with the same friends on the same roads. The roads are now more congested, jammed with traffic, spotted with traffic lights, cut by intersections and lined with urban clutter. Yet, in the mess, we can still escape. We continue to grow in profound ways, as we once did as teens, yet now we are husbands, fathers, employees and professionals, with greater obligations and purpose. Even after years of separation, only a few minutes pass before I feel as though not a day has gone by since we rode side by side as boys. There's no awkwardness of acquaintances reunited; we resume where we left off, even though our lives are so different on every level. Marcel, a friend I have ridden with since we were very young boys, told me he thinks we remain close, despite time and distance, because the experiences we had together were profoundly life-changing and created an everlasting bond.

Riding decades ago out of the city on warm spring days, we snaked through lines of cars that idled in traffic, stuck on the city's main arteries. I imagined their drivers listening to radios for the traffic reports, becoming increasingly infuriated as they thought of the still-distant sanctity of their homes, their time being wasted in a mess of similar cars that formed a trail of brake lights leading to the next traffic light. A sinuous route through the back streets took us away from the fumes and horns and into open air and greenery. We ventured to places few of those living in the city had ever seen. We used the sun to gauge how much longer we could ride before it became dangerously dark and our parents began to worry. On the way home, we would stop at a gas station, pooling our money to buy chocolate bars and Cokes to share. With the zap of sugar we raced each other over the final kilometres. At night, I lay in bed, listening to Led Zeppelin, Pink Floyd or Beatles records, humming to the tune with a sense of fulfilment that nothing else could give. Cycling gave depth to my life that was inexplicably profound and pure.

The weekend races were thrilling adventures, where we would meet our rivals from past weekends. We were all friends, even the riders with whom we would spar in the finale, rubbing elbows and racing for a tight line into a hairpin bend where the first rider in is almost guaranteed to win. Accidents and errors were forgiven and forgotten, perhaps because there was a mutual understanding that we were all learning, or perhaps because we were too young to hold a grudge. The stakes weren't what they would be when sport became a career. As boys and teens, nobody told our small tribe in blue and white that we needed to train each evening after school or that we could improve our race results. Our desire to ride and to push ourselves was purely internal. We didn't race for trophies or the handful of dollars we might win. Not every boy I raced with and against felt the same way, however. A few were driven to hate cycling by their misguided parents.

My first season as a junior was successful. I won or placed on the podium in most of the races I rode and began competing internationally. I signed up for every race my parents could get me to. With a small group of clubmates, who also became my best friends, they drove us across the province, into Quebec and through the northeastern United States. I raced on the road, the grass track, the velodrome and the dirt. My training had little structure. I sprinted against my mates for the tops of hills and town signs. We stayed out on our bikes until it was dusk and arrived home to worried parents and cold dinner.

In the summer of 1991, before my sixteenth birthday, and midway through my first season as a junior, my life and the way I saw sport changed. There was progression and digression.

Mirek Mazur, a Polish immigrant to Canada, was hired as the coach of my province's team in Ontario. I first met him at the Provincial Time Trial Championships. My mother had driven me to the course in our red Kia van. To me, time trials fell into a secondary category of bike races. Solo time tests lacked the allure and energy of the road race: a large peloton racing through the countryside and stampeding into towns, sprinting, surging, attacking and splintering. The time trial is a controlled effort with few variables, making it a pure test in which weakness is readily apparent. A rider can't hide in the slipstream of another to conserve his energy. There are few tactics.

Although I didn't know it at the time, Mirek was there to select the riders he could develop to race on the provincial team. He was after raw talent or 'big engines', his name for physically talented athletes.

Several dozen cars were parked in a gravel parking lot. Absinthe-green fields surrounded us. A few farmhouses sheltered by a copse of trees spotted the horizon. We could have been anywhere in southern Ontario. Trees, fields, open rolling roads and not much else. The course was just as predictable: twenty kilometres on a straight road, a U-turn at a pylon placed on the yellow line in the middle of the road and twenty kilometres back. I had ridden dozens of similar time trials over different distances since I was a boy. Even though I didn't enjoy time trials as much as road racing, I'd been immersed in the cycling culture since birth, and I knew they were an elemental discipline within the sport. I had to ride them if I wanted to become a pro.

As I pinned my numbers to my skinsuit – the tight-fitting Lycra one-piece we used for short-distance events – in the back seat of the van I scanned the parking lot, making a mental note of my rivals. Not that it made any difference. In a time trial I simply had to ride as hard as I could over the entire distance. Most were familiar faces that I had seen every weekend, or sometimes more frequently, throughout the racing season. Fathers pumped tyres. Sisters sat on coolers. Riders stretched, trying to quell their nervous energy. Moms chatted. Some snapped photographs. Iron Maiden boomed out of the lousy speakers of a senior rider's silver Honda Accord. His teammates sat in his car with their shirts off and their legs out the door, readying themselves for the race. The music was intended to amplify their spirits before a fierce effort, but it seemed to annoy everyone else in the parking lot. Nobody said anything. Every weekend followed the same routine.

There was one person I didn't recognise. Blond, with a baseball cap pulled low over his eyes but resting high on the back of his head, he stood out from the rest. Stocky and fairly short, but fit, he didn't socialise but appeared to analyse the scene. Assuming he was a rider's father, I didn't pay much attention to him.

Pre-race nervousness made me feel skittish and nauseated. I'd picked at my breakfast and the food wasn't sitting well. The focus on the race, the result and everything I couldn't control had drained my desire for food.

Numbers pinned on, I squirmed into my skinsuit and buckled up my helmet. To avoid puncturing the silk time-trial tubular tyres, I walked my bike across the gravel lot to the start line. My hand shook slightly with nervousness as I guided and pushed my bike by the handlebar stem.

In a misguided effort to control my nerves, I asked a key rival, as I did before every race, if he was going to win. We both laughed, nervously.

His answer: I bet you will.

Mom was there to wish me good luck. Everything else became a blur.

Within moments, I was off on my own, searching for my rhythm, hearing my breath, the rushing wind and the whirl of my tyres on the tarmac. As the effort enveloped me, I found clarity in my focus. My pre-race anxiety vanished. My legs, the bike and my lungs moved freely and in synch, allowing me to push the pedals even harder.

Passing rivals who had started minutes ahead, I knew I was moving quickly. Crossing the finish line, I freewheeled, releasing the tension my legs had sustained for just under an hour.

I rode across the gravel parking lot, now unconcerned with puncturing or mishap. The man with the low-slung cap and the blond hair approached me. I was still panting, with my head hung low. My arms felt weak as I grasped the bars. I had drained every bit of energy from my body. My muscles felt seared with lactic acid. My lungs seemed torn from the effort, and I hacked a dry cough. I could taste the familiar metallic flavour of blood.

From his broken English, I could tell he was from Eastern Europe. His platinum-blond hair said Poland.

Do you want to race for the provincial team?

Yes. Why?

I'm the coach. We are meeting at the track in Delhi this week for some training.

Okay. But I have school.

I had never missed a class for a bike race. Now I sensed the expectations were shifting.

In the late 1970s and '80s many Eastern European athletes and coaches defected to North America and took coaching positions with the national organisations. In Canada, most cycling coaches were European immigrants. Unlike most Canadians, they had grown up immersed in cycling, and they had a profound understanding and knowledge of the sport.

These coaches' hardened characters and demanding work ethic produced results. Edward Borysewicz, the controversial US national team coach, became a guru whose training programmes and guidelines were followed religiously by a generation of coaches and cyclists. Eddy B, as he was known, led many US cyclists to medals at the 1984 Olympics in Los Angeles, although several later admitted to blood doping, a practice that was still not illegal at that point. Many of the cyclists coached by Eddy B became top professionals, while he moved on to work for professional teams. The knowledge that eastern Europeans brought to North American Olympic sport in the 1980s was fundamental. In a society where sport was military-based, they had devised tough training systems. The most resilient rose to the top, surviving the training and going on to win medals, while the rest returned to their hometowns to work in the factory or the bakery.

Now I was a provincial team member, and Mirek became my coach. I felt excited to have a proper coach, a European. He had coached national champions who had gone on to become professionals. Being on the team took me a step closer toward my own goal of joining them. There was no planning involved. I had never mapped out my career, the progressive steps, or tried to figure out how I would get to the Tour de France. I rode, had fun, and assumed that if I won I would achieve my aims. I didn't obsess over my training or the races I should ride. Cycling was a hobby and a game. Riding was playing.

Like all adolescents, I found my wings. As a teenager on a bike I flew to places I never knew existed, discovering people, places, ideas and myself. It was my first real sense of independence. There were no external expectations. Young and naive, I thought it was all fun. I skied. I ran. I played hockey. I skateboarded. I was moving nonstop, sweating, laughing and enjoying it. On the bike, there was an internal pressure to win that was rooted in a desire and a dream. But I had little understanding of what I was doing or why I won.

Naivety was bliss. That changed when I was invited to race for the provincial team. This was different. At the provincial level, training wasn't really training but a test of our abilities. I could hear it in Mirek's voice and see it in his mannerisms. I wasn't accustomed to judgement. Selection had never been a concern.

Mirek told me I didn't train properly or hard enough. I told him that I ran, skied and played hockey through the winter. Terse and demeaning, he asked if I was a hockey player or a cyclist. To be a cyclist I had to devote myself to the bike.

The next season I followed his training programme. The year began with a two-week training camp in Florida that spanned my birthday, Christmas and New Year's Eve. It was the first time I had been away from my family for a significant event or holiday. At the camps and through the spring, I learned to train in structured blocks established to achieve goals. When it was well below freezing we rode up and down climbs to stay warm and to accomplish the required workload for the session. In the summer, when I wasn't in school I was often riding three times a day: before breakfast I rode the rollers, progressively increasing my effort over thirty minutes to warm up my body and burn fat; later in the morning I did a hard road ride or track session with intense intervals; in the late afternoon I was scheduled to ride for one to two hours at a steady tempo. When I wasn't on my bike I was either eating or lying down. The sessions on the bike remained fun when I rode with teammates. At home, they were drills I felt obliged to complete. No longer was I a kid on a bike. I often felt like an adult in a factory.

The training camps in small towns in Pennsylvania, South Carolina and California were like boot camps. We stayed in unfurnished apartments, often for weeks or months, sleeping on air mattresses, three to a room, six to an apartment. The spartan apartments were the cheapest to be found. In Ramona, California, a SWAT team surrounded the condo development and raided our neighbours in force with machine guns out. A methamphetamine lab was revealed, and our neighbours, whom we had rarely seen, were led away in handcuffs. In Kutztown, Pennsylvania, we went to bed with the odour of pizza baking in the restaurant below and the pounding of drums as our neighbour hammered a beat to quell his frustration after a heated argument with his girlfriend. Because we were tired-out cyclists, we built a rope hoist to lift our groceries from the van up the three flights to our apartment.

We slept, we cooked and we trained. This was the rhythm we adapted to. We became accustomed to the process of training towards a goal, racing, and then repeating. It was an adventure that matured us in ways I only began to realise later in my life. We learned to navigate the world in the compressed environment of a team on the road. We had each invested heavily in cycling. Teammates went from race to race, depending on their winnings of a hundred or two hundred dollars, never more than a thousand, to eat and stay south in a warm climate for another week or two. To maintain balance, to avoid cracking and failing, we had to keep moving, pushing our bodies, racing hard and trying to win. Each race we rode was an opportunity to gain fitness, win some money, and be seen by a higher-calibre team that might offer us a job or at least cover our expenses.

We saw all of North America as we followed the sun from place to place, from race to race, from the winter in the southwest to the summer in Pennsylvania and New York. The long hours in the car and the even longer hours on the bike brought me closer to my teammates. With time they became my best friends. We animated each other to get up and ride; together the training was more manageable.

To offset the structured sessions, we set out on adventures when Mirek was away, or when we had an easier day, when we were free to roam. During those rides we had fun, cruising the countryside and turning a ride into a playful adventure. Such moments punctuated the training routine, allowing us to branch off from our scheduled routines and play like boys.

Away at a training camp in Trexlertown, Pennsylvania, we spent most of the summer in an empty apartment, without a television and with relatively little furniture. Wooden bottle crates made night tables. We cranked up a stereo that we had packed in the van from Toronto and, with nothing else to do but read, chat or write, we taught ourselves to bake bread. To avoid draining ourselves further in the heat of the afternoon, we saved the third and most intense training session of the day for the evening, after the sun had set and the air had cooled. It was also the preferable time to have the oven baking. As the bread rose, we thrashed out intervals on our 'death machines', modified Monarch stationary bicycles devised to simulate intense track sessions, using a weighted wheel to increase the workload. The Beastie Boys or Nirvana thumped and wailed in the background as we spun away, huffing, puffing, grunting and soaking the patio in sweat.

During that period, away at the camps, living in dingy housing, I often woke with less desire to ride as fatigue set in. To be good and, most importantly, to win, I had to climb on my bike each morning and complete the specified dose of training. The obligation to ride was new to me. Now I played games on the bike less frequently than I had when I was younger. There was joy in our friendships, but the constant physical pressure that we applied to ourselves was draining, and the expectations weighed heavy.

The training was some of the toughest I did during my career. More than physically wearing, it was mentally exhausting. Mirek pushed us hard and rarely seemed satisfied with the results unless we won convincingly. At the velodrome in Trexlertown, my father, who had come along to help out, became upset with the way Mirek treated me after I'd finished second in a race against much older riders. Mirek told my father that I should have won, that I was the strongest, but I'd made stupid tactical errors. Such negativity helped all of us grow stronger and perform, but I lost something important in the process: the innocence of a boy who loved his sport. At the time, I didn't realise this. I pushed on towards the goal. And my life changed.

I have spent my winters on the bike every year since I was sixteen. From that year on, every other activity became secondary to cycling or was done solely to enrich my strength on the bike. Base fitness, the foundation for the racing season, is built by riding for hours at a steady speed. As our fitness develops, we can mentally and physically assume greater workloads and the intensity of the training increases. Then we are ready to race. We start the season with a blank canvas, and then progressively lay down a foundation with changing stimulus. At the end of the season, there are spots of effervescence under layers of work.

This has been my routine. Depending on climate and environment my training changed slightly, but there was always a daily goal. Once I had graduated from high school, that goal overwhelmed almost everything else in my life. In Toronto, I gave up hockey and rode in the ice, snow or wet slush, and I spent hours on the home trainer. When I lived in Colorado, I skied, hiked and rode high above the tree line on dirt roads in the mountains. In Catalonia, where every season suits a cyclist, I did nothing outdoors but ride. The increasingly longer racing season leaves little time for much else.

A racer counts the days until the end, ticking them off like a prisoner in a cell. We count down everything we do. A racer's life is the constant pursuit of a goal. To push ourselves to extremes we are always looking beyond the present. Our bodies move in the moment, but our minds are two steps ahead.

Ever since my first stage competition, my daily race routine has involved pulling out the race book in my hotel room before bed and analysing and memorising the details of the course. It was much like I did as a boy when I had to learn poems for school. I believed that if I read the course details before bed, they would spin through my mind in my sleep and, by the morning, would be etched in my memory.

During the races we are constantly counting down our lives. Our cyclocomputers tell us how many kilometres we have covered, so we calculate how many are left. The directeurs remind us over the race radio how many kilometres there are until a climb, a corner, a windy section, an intermediate sprint, a town, and the finish. The markers are both tactical and psychological. The race will play out on certain sections of course. Broken down into segments, a tough task becomes far more manageable. A 220-kilometre stage with five climbs is daunting on paper, so we mentally trick ourselves: 'Only two climbs are really hard, there is a long section of flat in the middle, today is the last hard day of racing and tomorrow is easier . . .'

And when we finish a stage race, we start working towards the next one. Along the way we tick boxes as objectives and targets are achieved. We are constantly working towards improvements, setting greater goals once we have achieved the first ones and recalibrating after missing others.

In training, we count down the hard days until the easier ones, the number of intervals left in a training session, and the number of minutes and then seconds left in an interval. From the training camp on, riders break down the season, always looking towards the off season and the end, where they can take a brief break before starting all over again. That focus gives purpose and direction.

As a stage race wears on, riders find their position in the peloton based on their fitness level and health. Some meet their goals. Others don't come close and resign themselves to just getting through. They suffer in the hope that if they finish, they will rest, recover and rebound and reach a higher peak in fitness from the sustained daily effort over three weeks, a peak that would be impossible to achieve through training.

During the race, the riders talk about what they look forward to when the race ends. Some talk about an alcohol-fuelled night out with their girlfriend, friends or wife. For others, it is food, a gluttonous feast like they haven't eaten in months, and for others it is a few days on the beach. Almost everyone simply looks forward to a week without the obligation to ride.

Our desire to ride soon returns though. We need the effort, the routine and the release.

Whatever our daily suffering, every rider in the race holds on to a shred of hope and belief. Maybe tomorrow will be our lucky day, where everything will go right, and we will find ourselves in a breakaway that will beat the odds and forge ahead, to win. We push and keep pushing to get through the tough days, praying, hoping and knowing from past experience that there are better days to come. A bicycle race waits for nobody. If we waver for too long or break down, we fall outside the imposed time limit. The race rolls on and we go home. Weakness isn't tolerated. This is the work ethic Mirek instilled.

Mirek worked hard for his athletes and was proud of his and our success. Our victories added to his résumé and to ours. On many training rides he rode with us. His love for his job and for the bike was apparent as he pedalled along with us or stood in the track centre and recorded our times. Cycling was his vocation and he was devoted to it. His dreams, like ours, were rooted in cycling successes. But like a father who tries to teach his children with tough love only to damage their relationship forever, he caused many athletes to crack under the strain and quit racing. Those who stuck with it won medals or became professionals. Without Mirek, I might never have become a pro. The work ethic got me out of the door in blowing gales and lashing rains. It pushed me to complete workouts when all I really wanted to do was to ride home and sit on the sofa. With Mirek's influence, the guilt that ate at me through the day if I didn't get out and finish my tasks was much harder to endure than my efforts on the bike.

At the end of the training sessions, I felt something different from anything I had ever experienced before. The sense of completing a task beyond my perceived limits was overwhelmingly satisfying. The endorphin rush and release that naturally occurs with intense exercise produced a sense of elation, a natural high that I soon learned was addictive. I spent many of those sessions alongside Scott Hastie. We won national titles together and travelled the continent in an old van loaded with bikes. Recalling our time with Mirek, he wrote to me, 'I may be a bit crooked but some of my best memories in cycling come from the hard work it took to ever feel on top of things in races: Sweat-filled shoes on the death machine while on the balcony in Kutztown during a storm.'

Under Mirek's guidance, I progressed to Canada's national cycling team, then over to Europe, where I raced for the first time in Italy, Germany and France. I was ready to race against the best in the world.

9

In the back of the team car, I worked on a crossword puzzle with my teammate Mat Anand as we jerked and swerved through the rush-hour traffic in Bergamo. The blasting horns and cars passing centimetres from one another didn't bother me, yet I didn't feel at ease in the back seat. The car threaded its way through the narrow cobbled streets and into a town square, where we could hear an emcee's voice echoing off the thick stone walls of the ancient buildings.

In the spring of 1996, I was thrilled to be in Italy, with the Canadian national team. I felt ready for the challenging stage race, the Settimana Bergamasca. It was an event Lance Armstrong had won when he was a neo-professional in 1991, but I had no real idea of what to expect. This would be the first time I had ridden with top professionals. Of the teammates with me, five would go to the Olympics in Atlanta. I was twenty, the youngest on the Canadian team. This was an opportunity, as nobody expected much from me. I had little experience in Europe. The rest of the team had spent seasons overseas, with amateur clubs in France or with the national team.

Denis Roux, our coach, thought the peloton would be filled with national teams and lower-tier professionals, and he expected our team to win a stage or two. He had made it clear to the more experienced riders on the team that he would be disappointed with anything less.

We pulled in at the end of a long line of team cars, each spotless, with bright coloured logos painted on every surface.

The Canadian car contrasted with the rest, with a few sponsor logos and a red maple leaf on the side panels and hood. From cycling magazines, I recognised the logos of pasta manufacturers, construction, cement and glass companies and wine producers. With their legs stretched out of the open car doors or propped on the doorframes, the riders waited to be called to the podium and introduced to the small crowd that had gathered in the square. Each rider was overdressed, with his tracksuit top zipped up to his neck and long pants, despite the warm spring weather. A few children milled around the team cars asking for autographs, team caps, musettes and bottles. Only five years had passed since I was one of them. In my bedroom in Toronto, the walls were still plastered with posters, team stickers and caps. In the bedside table drawer I kept an autograph book filled with my heroes' signatures, several of whom I could now see in their team cars.

The emcee's animated voice blasted names out of the speakers: Leonardo Piepoli, Pavel Tonkov, Stefano Faustini, Gianni Faresin. The list went on. Many of the names I had heard while watching top-level races on television. Only a few national teams were presented to the public, which meant we were up against some tough professional competition. The race was going to be much harder than Denis had anticipated. I had no great expectations. I was a neophyte who was here to learn. For me nothing changed when we were surrounded by top pros. I was just starstruck.

Back at the hotel, staring at the ceiling while I lay in bed, I watched the beams of passing car lights cut through the darkness of the room. Seconds later, the drivers would honk their horns, alerting oncoming drivers as they blazed up the narrow mountain road and screeched their tyres through the switchbacks. I was too young to let cars or light keep me awake. Thoughts of the race had my mind churning. The race book, which every rider in almost every race is given before the start, outlined the stages, the courses, the climbs, the rules and the prize money. I had reread it a half dozen times before I turned off the lights, trying to grasp how hard the race was going to be and how I would fare. I had no clue. The photos of past champions, climbing to victory and receiving kisses on the podium, didn't help much. The race looked a lot harder than anything I had done before. I had never raced up a real mountain. Now I had to do it in a peloton of top professionals.

At dinner we ate too much Italian pasta. Denis scolded us, as if we were misbehaving school children. Before we arrived at the table he had already removed the jugs of juice, saying it was full of sugar that we didn't need. The pasta was better than anything I had ever eaten. All of us ate as if it was our last meal. The hotel was a simple two-star, like so many others I would stay in through the rest of my cycling career. The tiled rooms were clean and austere, with none of the frivolities of a North American room. With two small single beds, white sheets, a blanket, white towels, two simple bedside tables, two lights and shutters, it felt more like a room in a hospital than a hotel. As my career progressed I grew to appreciate the simplicity of such rooms and their cleanliness.

On the start line the next day, the difference between pro and amateur was obvious. The kilometres that the pros had ridden and the hundreds or thousands of races were apparent in their demeanour and physique. I gazed at their bikes, spokes, wheels and legs, still starry-eyed to be there. Everything from their new tyres to their gelled hair set them apart from us. The amateurs' clothing was faded and mismatched, while theirs had been tailored to perfection. Each of their bikes looked as if it had come directly from a shop. Ours looked worn, with scratches, faded leather saddles and last year's dated equipment. There was even a notable contrast between European and North American professionals. In America, the racing isn't as hard or mountainous, and the riders are heavier. The demands chisel the Europeans.

The professional riders appeared amazingly calm. They seemed to feel no pre-race nervousness. Their calmness reflected their experience, their professionalism. They knew their places, their potential and their roles. The nervousness that the rest of us felt reflected our insecurity about our ability. Such emotion is not absent from the professional peloton, especially prior to key races, but after riding thousands of races, the pros know the routine.

The tension in us, the amateurs, was evident. Our heads were filled with questions that we were about to answer for ourselves. While waiting for the town mayor to cut the start ribbon and the starter's pistol to fire, my teammate shook his foot clipped into his pedal, as if he were tapping away to a beat in his head. Another yawned, and a third adjusted his brakes.

The race began. I hid in the belly of the peloton, sucked along in the slipstream, constantly aware of the riders around me and their movements. In a peloton of professionals, I felt like a misfit and was more cautious than normal, trying not to bump elbows with other riders or make a juvenile error. I wanted to be one of them. As the race went on I heard yells of 'Amateur', followed by Italian obscenities from the professionals as they called out a young inexperienced rider for a manoeuvre that nearly caused a crash.

The first attacks and surges in the peloton felt no fiercer than in any other race I had ridden. But there was a fluidity to the race that I had not felt before. The pro teams controlled the race, almost as if there was a truce between them, allowing the amateur riders to attack and a small breakaway of just a handful of non-contenders to forge a gap. I didn't feel the abrupt slowing and surging of amateur racing. The peloton cruised along at a steady speed under a tempo imposed by the pro teams' domestiques. They rode on the front of the group with vigilance, reeling in large breakaways and reining in effervescent attacks that disturbed their rhythm. Once the breakaway had disappeared up the road, the lead teams forced a slower tempo and the peloton settled. Rivals chatted like old friends. Others dug into their pockets for a bit of food to eat. Some moved to the back of the peloton, one arm in the air, to call for their team car. I looked around at the mountain peaks in the distance.

For an hour the gap to the breakaway grew, and then, like a conductor shifting the tempo of his orchestra, a rider from Panaria, one of the pro teams, moved to the front and progressively lifted our speed, beginning what would be a long pursuit. It was a rhythm of racing that was new to me, contrasting with almost everything I had experienced before.

As we drew closer to the finish, the tempo continued to increase. The change was subtle. With each climb, the peloton thinned further. We had gone from a bubble of riders to one long thin line as each rider fought to diminish his workload by keeping in the slipstream of the rider in front of him. The team on the front rode in a tight formation, in unison, each knowing his role, his limit and his objective.

The peloton caught the breakaway and passed them as if they were in a different race. Their speed seemed to be half of ours. The peloton was moving along like a flywheel that had gained momentum over the course of the day.

About ten kilometres from the foot of the final ascent, there was a sudden surge in the group. Teams in formation began racing for the front and fighting for the lead position. Behind, there was panic as every rider realised that he needed to be in position behind the lead teams. If he wasn't, he had no chance of winning or placing. The once controlled peloton was now in frenzy. Teammates yelled commands at each other to speed up, slow down, move left or right. Rivals screamed obscenities. It seemed we couldn't go any faster. Not far from my physical limit, everything at the roadside and beyond was now a blur as I focused on the road ahead and the movement of the riders. As we sped through the towns, there were crashes as riders overlapped wheels and clipped parked cars or signposts. Brakes screeched, riders yelled, crashes disrupted the flow of the peloton momentarily, like a rock dropped into a river. The pursuit of the line now overwhelmed everything else. A kilometre from the final ascent the speed lifted again, and then we slammed on our brakes, skidding as we turned into the climb. As I accelerated out of the corner, in the middle of the group, the leaders were already far ahead, out of their saddles, soaring uphill. I tried to match the pace, but soon realised it was futile.

Within metres, everything was again calm as each rider sank into his own effort, trying to find a tempo he could maintain until the top. No longer were we a peloton but individuals and small scattered groups, each trying to find the best and easiest line up the mountain. There was nowhere to hide now. Slipstream had little effect on a climb. Some riders, knowing their job was done, rode within themselves, while others like me put every bit of energy into the pedals. I still didn't know any other way to race.

Nearing the finish I could hear the emcee bellowing riders' names as they crossed the line. Spectators lined the road, cheering us on. Over the last metres I punched at my pedals, squeezing every last bit of energy from my body. Finishing, I swerved slightly as my body relaxed, unclipped from my pedals, let my legs dangle like limp pieces of meat, and coasted to a stop to rest my head and arms on the handlebars. Panting, I tried to slow my breath so that I could take a sip of water from my bottle.

Driven by Denis to the hotel, I sat in the back seat of the team car, my legs aching and twitching. I ate a prosciutto and buffalo mozzarella sandwich – the soigneurs had prepared them that morning for each of us. Looking for something else to eat, I found some cookies under the front seat. As I opened the packet, Denis asked what I was doing, making it clear cyclists shouldn't be eating cookies. They were his and the mechanic's. I put them back and sipped on my water bottle.

The next stages pushed me to my physical limits. The leading teams never relented, shredding the peloton with their fearsome tempo and exploding it in the mountains. But I held on far longer than most, until the main protagonists made their final attacks. The professionals yelled at me on occasion for being in their midst at the front. Like a fly or a bee, I was perhaps annoying to them, getting in the way of the job they had to do. Or perhaps it was because young Canadian amateurs weren't supposed to be in the front towards the end of a hard race in the mountains. Each day, I dug deeper than I ever had before to stay with the leaders. As the race went on, I slept less and less, my heart pounding as it tried to help my body recover, my muscles twitching from the damage and my bum raw with saddle sores. This was what it felt like to race with professionals.

Through the week I held my position in the first twenty-five riders in the overall classification. As we climbed the mountain passes I held on to the peloton that had been whittled down to two dozen. Unable to stick with the final attacks, I was dropped, and then, with every ounce of energy left, I raced over the last kilometres of the stages to the finish line. My teammate Peter Wedge, who was a few years older and more experienced, helped me to stay with the group on a mountain pass, pacing me and encouraging me. I didn't realise how much I was suffering until he looked over as we neared the summit to ask if I was okay; it wasn't his words that made me aware but the expression of concern.

On the final mountain climb, on the second to last day of the race, I realised I could compete with the best. In the front group of twenty or so riders, I sat in the back with two of my teammates and held on. If I could make it over the last climb with the leaders, I would move up in the classification.

As we passed through a valley, the leader of the King of the Mountains competition tapped me on the shoulder. I looked at him. He pointed to a mountain in the distance, then tilted his hand up, his fingers pointing towards the sky, showing me the gradient. He then pointed to my freewheel and waved his finger back like a teacher telling his student he had done something wrong, indicating that my gearing wasn't sufficient to climb the mountain. I looked around at the other bikes in our small group. They all had big cogs on the back and small chain rings on the front. I would have to grind and swerve my way up the hill. The fact that the rider acknowledged my presence in the group and warned me of what we were approaching was something. Perhaps he had seen me fighting to stay with the group over each pass and had taken pity on me, or perhaps, having been up front each day, I was no longer just another face in the peloton. Somehow, a small gesture from a top rider made me feel accepted.

The ascent he had pointed out was steeper than I had imagined, and the road was far narrower. In the first few hundred metres the leaders pulled away, and the group splintered into ones and twos behind them. The road laced its way up the mountain, a line of switchbacks to the top. One by one the team cars passed me, their exhaust thick and dark as the engines strained with the gradient. There was no fluidity to my pedal stroke. I could feel each revolution as if I were in a gym pushing weights with my legs. I used my entire body to keep the bike moving and searched for the easiest line. A rider passed me holding on to his team car, something I had never seen before. As my career progressed I would become accustomed to it. Riders cheated as soon as they were out of sight of the commissaires, tacking themselves onto the cars or motorcycles or encouraging the spectators to push them up the climbs. It was often those at the back, who were struggling the most, who used the cars just to make it to the finish. At times, when courses were exceptionally hard or competitors injured, the officials turned a blind eye to a tow or a push and allowed an inconsequential rider a reprieve from the suffering.

Looking over my shoulder up the mountain, I was convinced it would have been easier to climb off and hike straight up it with my bike on my shoulder. The final kilometre seemed to last five minutes or more. Over the top, I accelerated, descending like a madman, chasing the leaders, skidding through corners and charging down the straights, a fearless kid with nothing to lose. At the finish, I was drained and elated. Sitting on a kerb, my bike beside me on the tarmac, I sipped from my water bottle, stretched out my legs and closed my eyes as a feeling of contentment washed over me.

That night, as they had every other night, my teammates chatted at the dinner table about the speed of the race, how abnormal and inhuman it seemed. The Australians, the only other foreign amateur team in the race, sat across from us in the hotel dining room and shared similar stories and thoughts. Naive and not realising exactly what they were talking about, I had kept pushing, doing the best I could and discovering what I was capable of.

The final stage was the easiest, a short circuit race on the plains near Brescia, yet the pace was as furious as in the others. Rarely did my speedometer read under 50 kph and often it read over 60. Unable to sit comfortably on my saddle because of the sores, I counted the kilometres until the final finish line. I was now the best-placed rider on our team, so my teammates helped me out, fetching bottles and keeping me out of the wind. It was a position I had never been in and, being the youngest, it was a status I felt awkward assuming.

Crossing the line, I felt relief not only because the race was over, and I no longer had to sit uncomfortably in my saddle, but also because I knew I could compete with the best on tough terrain. I could persist with my dreams. At the finish line, the cars were quickly packed up. A van driven by the mechanic departed for the airport to drop off my teammates, who were returning to other European countries or flying back to North America. I was slightly jealous of those returning home. I still had a few months of races to ride in France before the Vélo Club Annemasse would allow me to return to Toronto. I drove back with Denis in the Canadian team car. He would drop me in Annemasse on his way to Nevers, south of Paris.

In the team car, a Peugeot Turbo, we flew home. The speedometer hovered near 160 kph. Still cars passed us. Speed limits seemed more of a suggestion than a law.

Denis was happy with my performance. During the drive, he dictated a short training programme for me to follow leading up to the next races. He also told me that I had a shot at making the Olympic team. Goosebumps rose on my skin and my stomach fluttered. He then dictated a list of medications I should buy at the pharmacy when I returned to Annemasse. As I wrote out the list, he explained what each would do: this will clean your liver after the race and help with recovery, and this will keep you healthy. They were all available over the counter. Yet this was the first time a coach had told me to take medication. I felt uneasy. Denis assured me I wouldn't test positive and that it would help my performance.

Soon after I had arrived in Annemasse, a month before the trip to Italy, I was taken to the Vélo Club doctor for a checkup. In France, as in most of Europe, each licensed rider must undergo a battery of tests to ensure he is healthy enough to race. The doctor also took blood, something I had never experienced before, to see if my blood values were all normal. Two weeks later, he prescribed iron tablets, magnesium and calcium and a multivitamin, because some were on the lower end of the normal range. This was a level of professionalism in amateur cycling I had never before experienced. Suddenly I was considering details I had never thought about.

Denis dropped me at my apartment, shook my hand and said he would be in touch. I put my bags down and sat on my bed. The pain of the race was still in my legs. They felt heavy and disconnected from the rest of my body, perhaps because they had been used far more than the rest of me. The chafing on my inner thigh from the chamois in my shorts rubbing tens of thousands of times as I pedalled through each stage now stung as I sat down, and the fabric of my tracksuit touched the open sores. Leaning back on the pillow, I dug out Denis's instructions, the training and medical advice. The afternoon sun shone through the white lace curtains. The compressor from the auto-body shop across the parking lot from the apartment revved, a noise I became deaf to with time. I put the scraps of paper on the bedside table, trading them for a crossword puzzle. Twirling the pencil in my hand, I felt content, yet concerned. I knew I could race with the best, but had no idea what it would take to continue the pursuit of my dreams.

Staring at the crossword my mind was elsewhere. The words weren't falling into place. But I had the time to figure it out.

10

Each race I rode felt as though it could be the one event that would give me the opening: one victory, on a hard course in front of the best amateurs and their directeurs, might result in a chance to race with a pro team. The chance was all I wanted. After that I would worry about the rest. Step by step.

In France, I saw every race as an opportunity. Even at the local races, where the results would only appear in the community newspaper and might be heard over the local radio, there might be a pro team directeur at the roadside. I targeted the bigger races, where the top ten finishers were often written up in the national sports paper, *L'Equipe*. I had been told that if my name appeared often enough, the pro teams would notice and eventually contact me. Christian Rumeau, the club's directeur sportif, who had worked in the pro ranks with the best teams and riders until he reached retirement age, told me that was how it would happen. It was how he had selected riders and how the directeurs who had once been apprenticed under him now selected their rosters.

The Circuit du Saône-et-Loire was a race I knew well. I had finished fourth in this race the year before. This year, I was expected to win.

The peloton had thinned under the pressure of the race. The course, which wound its way around the Saône-et-Loire *département*, was relentlessly sinuous and undulating; a route on which a rider in form felt at ease and someone out of shape cursed every rise and every corner. At the back, where the weakest rode, the pace was torturous. The elasticity of the peloton forced riders to sprint out of the corners to keep pace. The cold spring rain only deepened our misery. The 140 kilometres had whittled the group down to about thirty riders. Near the front, I rode behind the strongest, waiting for their attacks in the finale. It was the penultimate stage of a five-day race; this was the stage that would decide it.

Under the dark grey skies, the locals seemed to have disappeared into their homes. The narrow streets in the small towns were deserted as the peloton snaked from one end to the other. Smoke billowed from chimneys. The odour of onion soup wafted through as we raced past an old farmhouse. In the farm fields, tractors sank into the thick mud and small pools of water, and budding crops were buried in wetness.

The road went up gradually, not enough for a car driver to apply much more pressure to the accelerator, but enough that a cyclist could feel it in his thighs. It was an uncomfortable rise, where no gear seemed right. The rough tarmac only deadened the road, making my light aerodynamic carbon wheels feel ineffective and the high-pressure tubular tyres feel as if they were losing air. Halfway up the rise, just before the farm fields turned into dense forest, we passed the sign posted at the roadside that indicated twenty kilometres to go: over six kilometres uphill, six downhill and about eight false flat to the finish. Twenty kilometres was a golden number to a bike racer: the finish was near and the suffering would soon be over.

The weight of the road was wearing not only on me but on everyone else in the group. I could hear the deep panting of my rivals' breathing. Nobody was at ease. Some riders began moving on their bikes, struggling to find the extra power they needed to stay with the group. They shifted gears, up, down, up again, stood up, sat down and pulled on their handlebars as if they were pulling on reins, trying to make a tired horse gallop. The composure they had displayed only a few kilometres ago, when we sped through the small town, was gone. They were now paying for the futile attacks they had made on the last climb or even earlier in the race, when they were feeling fresh and confident.

Rumeau had told me not to move out of the wheels of the peloton and into the wind until the first of two switchbacks from the top of the final climb. At that point, which we were about to reach, he said I could attack. It couldn't be a half-hearted attempt, but one that would scorch my legs and lungs and would deliver the decisive blow to my rivals. Rumeau's tactical advice was never wrong. My legs told me I could do it. Nervous anticipation made me antsy to get to the first switchback.

In the group were the riders who had made the final selection weekly since the start of the year. There were few jerseys, bikes or faces I hadn't seen before. I could identify them in the peloton by their positions on their bikes and their pedal strokes.

One rider was unique. His platinum-blond hair contrasted with the brown and black hair of the others. Stockier than the slim Frenchmen, he looked, I thought, like a sprinter. He had won the previous stage, a massive group sprint, with ease. Yet now he was here with us in the hills, looking comfortable and confident. His garish yellow-and-red, faded and spattered Vélo Club Saint-Etienne jersey stood out in the group like a flag against the drab countryside. At breakfast, our mechanic had pointed him out in the buffet line and, with a wink, told me he had seen him riding the rollers at 8 a.m. Confused, I asked why he would be riding more than he had to during a stage race. I couldn't imagine adding kilometres to what was already a hard undertaking. The mechanic, who had once raced as a professional, told me he was riding the rollers to 'unblock' his body. I wasn't really sure what that meant. When I was a teen-ager, Mirek told us to ride the rollers before breakfast to lose weight and stimulate our bodies for the day's workout. But that meant a few hours on the track, not a 160-kilometre stage in the mountains.

From the mechanic's wink, I figured he was taking drugs and riding a little more on the rollers to sweat in hopes of elimi-nating their side effects. I had heard that cortisone made riders retain water, made them puffy, and if they didn't eliminate that excess water they would have to carry the excess weight through the stage or up the mountain, expending valuable energy that they should save for a potent, race-winning attack. But the roll-ers may simply have been this rider's way of warming up for the race.

In France, it seemed everybody was constantly talking about which riders were taking drugs. I didn't focus on the gossip, and the cultural gap helped to keep me isolated and innocent. Several times, I caught my teammates searching through my bags. When I asked them what the hell they were doing, they answered, as if it was a completely normal pastime, that they were looking to see what drugs I was taking. They had grown up in a culture where drugs were assumed to have fuelled every heroic performance. I grew up believing it was possible to win clean, that I could achieve my goals and dreams without drugs, and that I could beat the cheats. In high school I'd read the autobiography of the track sprinter Angella Issajenko, which detailed her use of drugs along with her Canadian teammate Ben Johnson. I'd read Paul Kimmage's book, *Rough Ride*, on his experiences with drugs in pro cycling. These books had not only shocked me, they'd made me aware of some of the realities in sport. But I thought the stories were isolated examples in a world of thousands of sportspeople. Like most spectators, I still wanted to believe that my heroes were clean, that only the few exceptions doped.

Those beliefs were eroded as I realised there was truth to the gossip. I began questioning every rider who beat me. After I finished second or sixth, my teammates or friends assumed everyone else was doped, and they often said, 'You were the real winner.' They meant it as a compliment, but I felt disheartened. I was racing to win, not to finish behind riders who might or might not be doped.

Even during the first season in France, I was stunned at the contrast in culture. I had grown up taking care of my body, believing that anything I put into it, from junk food, alcohol and tobacco to social drugs, would negatively affect my perfor-mance. It was how I was raised and what Mirek taught. I lived a monastic life, even as a teenager, when my high-school friends were partying late into the night. Now, in France, my ideals were upended.

After finishing third in a national level one-day race, I re-turned to the hotel. There was another one-day race the fol-lowing day, in another town close by. In a four-man breakaway, I had been beaten in a tactical battle by two riders from the same team, ASPTT Mulhouse. I had finished frustrated. My legs were good enough to win and still felt as if they had more to give. But tactics decided races more often than just legs. In the hotel dining room, we piled our plates high with pasta, being careful not to use too much oil, not to eat too much bread, and to fuel appropriately. Rumeau kept an eye on our consumption, commenting when we made an improper food choice.

As our plates were cleared from the table, I glanced across the room at the rivals from Mulhouse who had beaten me. They were pulling out cigarettes and lighting up. At first I thought I had to be mistaken, that they were mechanics and soigneurs and not riders. To be sure, I asked a teammate if they were racers or staff.

They're the guys who beat you, he answered.

They smoke?

Yes, to calm their nerves after the race.

I didn't really understand what that meant. I couldn't comprehend how guys who smoked had beaten me. Slowly, I began to realise just how different the cycling culture was from what I had perceived. In my second season, I became increasingly aware of doping and of races being bought, sold and controlled by le mafia, a group of veteran riders from different teams who rode together to ensure they won and that the prize money stayed within the group. They worked like mercenaries. Any rider could pay for their help to ensure a victory, and each region had its own mafia. In the heat of the summer, when the peloton became lazy and the public's attention was focused on the Tour, le mafia controlled the local races, which were often criteriums or circuit races with cash prizes. In France, even at the amateur level, cycling was not only sport but also a way to make a living.

Protected and sheltered by Rumeau, who was fully aware of the corruption even at the amateur level, I was fortunate not to have been completely immersed and misguided. He had told me that he would stop helping me if he heard of me doping or selling a race.

Earlier in the morning, during the team meeting, with the map opened on his bed in the dingy hotel room, Rumeau had explained how we should ride the queen stage of the Circuit de Saône-et-Loire. He pointed to each key section of the course on the map. He knew the climbs, and he told us about the gradient, the wind direction, and our rivals. After the meeting, I stayed behind. Rumeau gave me a photocopy of a section of the map with an X clearly marked at two points: one where the first major selection would occur, and one where I should attack.

Now, as we ascended, I counted the switchbacks. In each corner our tyres skidded as they struggled on the gradient to grip the wet gritty road. I had memorised the map in the team car on the way to the start. The road wasn't as I'd imagined it – it was narrower and darker under the grey skies and dense forest. Pine needles, cones, sand, stones and grit had washed onto the pavement. The group was smaller. Without looking back I could feel it by the shifting gears, the breathing and the sound of tyres crunching over the debris on the road. There couldn't be more than ten riders in the group. Four were in front of me, the rest were behind.

Since the morning, I had been thinking about the climb and the attack. The anticipation had built inside me during four hours of racing as I prepared myself for the surge and sprint to the finish line. The mental energy had accumulated, and I was ready to pounce. As we approached the critical corner, I moved slightly out of my rivals' slipstream to ensure I had a clean line ahead. I needed to move with subtlety so they couldn't predict the attack. Other riders had made their move on the lower slopes of the climb, but couldn't sustain their speed, and they were quickly reeled in. But everybody in the group knew there would be more attacks, and we eyed each other like animals studying their prey, gauging each movement and trying to predict the right moment to jump.

As we moved out of the corner, I jumped out of the saddle and punched the pedals with all the power I could produce. Initially, I didn't feel the burning pain of the effort in my legs and lungs. I could hear the shifting gears of my rivals as they accelerated to match my speed. Looking though my legs to my back wheel I could see nobody in my slipstream. It didn't matter. I had to commit to the road ahead, the climb and the finish line. I felt the pain from the effort as I neared the next switchback and the one-kilometre sign at the roadside that signalled the distance to the summit. My brain told me to ease off. I shut it down and persisted through the pain.

As I reached the summit, I came out of the forest. The road opened up and flattened. As if I was looking through a dirty window, my eyesight was blurred from the effort, the rain and the wind. In pouring rain, a rider can't see far ahead of him, and the intensity of his effort further inhibits his vision. In the distance the road dipped to the right, where the descent began. I slowed, sank lower on my bike and moved forward in my saddle, looking for power and trying to hide from the wind. I could sense that I was being caught. I eased up, releasing some of the pressure on my pedals and slowing my breathing. I looked around. Three riders were on my wheel. One of them was the blond sprinter from the Vélo Club Saint-Etienne. I moved into their slipstream to recover from the effort. My attack had failed. My body didn't have it. This wasn't how it was supposed to end.

Just before the corner, I eased out of the slipstream and surged to the left of the group, sprinting into the corner and the descent. Having spent my youth racing city-centre circuits with tight corners, I was fearlessly confident I could ride down the wet descent faster than my rivals. I accelerated out of the corner, sprinting again, and glanced over my shoulder. There was a significant gap between the others and me. I sped through the next corner, barely touching my brakes. My bike skidded slightly on the wet tarmac. The gradient became more acute, increasing my speed with each metre. My eyes, full of road grit, watered in the air rushing past my face. This was it. I was going to win.

But when I flew into the switchback, I knew I'd miscalculated. I touched my brakes, but the bike began to slide over the pebbles that had washed onto the apex of the turn. The bike slid out from under me as if I had ridden over marbles on a hardwood floor. Before I could react, I hit the ground. Adrenaline was pulsing through me.

As I moved to get up, the trio of followers passed me. Having seen me crash they had slowed down and were cautiously turning. One rider, a veteran who had spent a year or two racing on a small pro team, looked over and said in French, 'That will teach you to race downhill.'

My team car parked on the shoulder, the bumper a few feet from my head. The mechanic emerged from his nest of spare wheels and tools in the back seat to fix my bike. Rumeau jumped out to help me. Several other riders raced by, looking over their shoulders at the damage. The handlebars straightened, the bike was ready to go. But as I put my leg over the top tube an intense pain made me feel sick to my stomach. Pushing through it, I climbed onto the bike. Rumeau encouraged me, honking the horn with enthusiasm. There was still a chance I could regain contact with the leaders on the run into the finish. The pain intensified. I'd never felt such pain. I'd felt the sting of scrapes, grazes and cuts when I'd reached a finish line and the adrenaline of the race had abated. But the pain I felt now, in my left hip, made each pedal stroke excruciating. I pressed on, passing several of the riders. As I entered the final straight to the finish line, I could see the winner, several hundred metres ahead of me, raising his arms in the air. His jersey was yellow and red.

In the team car, I wanted to throw up from the pain. Sitting felt worse than pedalling. My clothing was in tatters, ripped by the road, stained with blood, grey from the rain and spotted with sand. A gaping hole in the flesh of my elbow was filled with dirt, muck and a piece of straw. Pulling back my shorts, I could see the bloody gouges in my left hip. Goosebumps covered my arms and legs, more likely from the shock than the cold.

Metres away from our car, the winner collected his flowers. I didn't care. As I sat in the front seat with my head braced against the window, my teammates changed in the back. I bit my lip, fighting back tears. They talked about the victor, Alexander Vinokourov, a Kazakh, who seemed unbeatable. They spoke about him as if he was something greater than a cyclist, something they would never be. Their compliments seemed loaded with competitive jealousy.

Rumeau moved around outside, chatting with old friends and other directeurs, unaware of the pain I felt. I'd finished only seconds behind the winner, and he still believed I was in the hunt for the overall win. I would at least have gained some precious points to ensure the team didn't drop in ranking. In the car, I felt caught, like a wounded animal in a trap. I wanted to run away, screaming in pain, in frustration and in sadness, but in front of my teammates I bottled up my emotions and remained quiet. I sat patiently, clenching my fists as the hot air from the car's heater blew against the open wounds, touching the open nerves, stinging like a hundred bees.

During the car ride to the hotel I closed my eyes, hoping it was over but not wanting to admit it to my teammates or myself. With each bump in the road I felt a shock of pain through my leg. The riders in the back seat chatted about the race and devoured ham sandwiches. None of it meant anything to me. I still wore my wet clothing. The pain had made it impossible to remove. Someone had draped my team tracksuit top over my shoulder and pulled a woolly hat over my head.

In the hotel, the pain intensified even further. I couldn't walk without a crutch or a teammate's support. I showered, cleaning the wounds with a plastic brush and antiseptic. I tried hard to keep a brave face. As I hobbled to dinner, a rival who had been in the breakaway with me consoled me, shaking his head as he saw my condition.

Before bed, a team soigneur, who was also a homeopath, gave me a handful of arnica to swallow for the pain. Through the night, I soaked the bed in sweat. Beside me in our small room, my teammate lay silently asleep, recovering from the race and preparing for another day. Unable to walk, I crawled to the bathroom to pee. From one shuffle to the next, I lay on the floor, resting and readying myself for the next painful movement.

The next morning, Rumeau did not want to believe I was in such pain and unable to race. He urged me to join the team for breakfast. I told him I couldn't move, let alone race. With the help of my roommate, he carried me to my bike to see for himself whether or not I could climb on. I couldn't lift my leg off the ground. It was over. I felt relieved that I didn't have to try.

Marcel, the president of the Vélo Club, and his wife drove me back to Annemasse. I asked to be taken directly to the hospital. An attractive young doctor reassured me that my leg was fine, that the bruising was causing the pain, and that X-rays weren't required. I limped home, unable to support my weight on the injured leg, but content that I could soon ride again.

The apartment I shared with a teammate was cold and damp. I turned up the heat, put on the kettle and pulled on a sweater. The pain in my leg pulsed with each movement. I balanced my weight against the wall, the railing and the chairs. With nothing in the fridge, I ate a bowl of cereal for dinner and sipped tea while doing a crossword puzzle that my mother had clipped from a Canadian newspaper, the *Globe and Mail*. The radio played an electronic dance tune, broadcast from ten kilometres away in Geneva. My bike rested against the wall in the front entrance, with my bag of race clothing beside it. I couldn't walk but I wanted to get back on.

Each night, I turned off the light and lay on the floor with my damaged leg elevated on the bed. It was the only way I could sleep. Anxious because I wasn't riding and unable to tolerate the pain any longer, I saw another doctor. He assured me it wasn't broken. When I asked him if I needed X-rays, he said no. If my leg was broken, he said, I would not be able to stand on it.

A week of sleepless nights passed. I tried to ride again. Idle in the apartment I was becoming increasingly uneasy.

In the apartment above me lived our landlord, Gérard Cheneval, his wife, Gabrielle, and their children, Raphael and Karen. They had been kind to me, cared for me and treated me like an adopted child. When I first arrived in Annemasse, they realised how lonely a foreigner living in a small town in France might feel. On the weekends, when I wasn't racing, they invited me to their country home or took me on day trips, which allowed me to experience life outside the cycling world. Knowing they were upstairs was reassuring, but as I had come overseas to ride and race, I felt unsettled and wanted to get moving.

Only moving and riding would ease my angst. I was missing key races that would affect my chances of becoming a professional. I was losing the fitness I had spent months trying to attain. I feared I would gain weight, putting me further behind my rivals.

Climbing on the bike was the hardest part. In the driveway, with one hand on the brick wall for stability and the other on the handlebar, I lifted my leg over the top tube, clipped into my pedals and pushed off. The pinch of the pedal stroke sent a shock of pain through my body, but amazingly I felt more comfortable on the bike than walking or sitting on the sofa or bed. I rode for an hour. Immediately I felt a release. My head felt clearer and everything seemed brighter. In a short loop through the countryside and down to the shore of Lac Léman, I had regained my lost freedom. The next day I rode for two hours, further increasing my sense of elation. By the end of the week, I was riding in the mountains on my usual training routes. My heart rate was thirty beats higher than it had been, but I disregarded it, happy to ride.

Not once did any of my coaches, massage therapists or doctors wonder if perhaps I had fractured my femur. When I asked, they said it wasn't possible. Naively, I trusted my advisers. As an athlete, my greatest fear was an injury that would slow the pursuit of my goals. All I wanted was to pedal.

So I rode. And then I raced. Five weeks later, I was winning again. Two months went by, and I was national champion. The possibility remained that I would sign a pro contract at the end of the season. My dream was alive. But my left leg still ached, and I was unable to match the power I had produced only months before.

Five months later, after another crash, I was back in the hospital. This time I had injured my back. Same story: no need for X-rays. 'You're okay. It's just bruising and muscle pain.'

I went to doctors and then chiropractors. Rumeau drove me to one appointment with a chiropractor. After the adjustment, I almost threw up. I felt dizzy, and I braced myself against Rumeau to keep from falling over. Two sleepless weeks went by. I tried riding. I was told I should race to get in shape for the Tour of Avenir, a key stage race for young riders, in which I was expected to perform and then sign a professional contract. I tried, but the pain was too great. I spoke on the phone about the injury with my parents. I told them I was in too much pain to perform, that I couldn't ride and that I had barely had a bowel movement in two weeks. My mother, who works in health care, told me to go to the radiology clinic and demand X-rays.

The technician told me he wouldn't X-ray me without a prescription. I explained I couldn't get one, because the doctor said it wasn't necessary. I said I would pay for the X-rays up front. The technician obliged. When he glanced at the images, I could see his surprise. He ordered me to take them to the emergency department immediately. I asked him to X-ray my hip while I was there. It had been bothering me for a few months, I said, and it was still causing me discomfort. I left the clinic with a pile of X-ray images, feeling sad and relieved. I now knew what was wrong: I had fractured three vertebrae and had a compression fracture through the neck of my femur.

In the ER, they were stunned to realise the images were mine. They immediately put me on a spinal board. Then they took me to a room and admitted me for the night. I had no idea how badly injured I was. In bed, I wondered if I could still ride in the World Championships. The doctors wanted to operate, but I wanted a second opinion. In fact, I really just wanted to get back to Canada. Once the doctor understood that I'd fractured my femur months earlier, he said I could return to Canada, without surgery, for further assessment.

Two days later, with my back immobilised in a corset, I flew to Toronto and went directly to the hospital to see specialists. Impatient, I asked the surgeon when I could race again. He explained that I was lucky to be walking. I had come within millimetres of being paralysed. Looking around the waiting room, my perspective shifted. My goals and dreams remained intact, but now I wondered if my body would allow me to achieve them.

11

Shifting into the big chain ring the bike began to move as it had six months ago, carrying me faster with each pedal stroke. My breathing, which only a few weeks ago had been laboured, almost panting, was once again fluid. Ascending the mountain, I had rediscovered the liberty the last crash had taken away from me. For months I had sat uncomfortably, trying to find the ease and power I had known all of my life. Biomechanically I was no longer the same, but with time I believed I could adapt. A bike had always felt like an extension of my body. Now my injuries had made it awkward to ride. I fidgeted and shifted my weight constantly to produce power.

I was told I would never be the same cyclist. The injuries had left me crooked. Like a car with a bent axle, I would never be able to travel at the high speeds needed to race professionally, and I would constantly run into biomechanical problems. I listened to the specialists and nodded, agreeing and understanding, but I already wanted to defy everything they said. I was a cyclist. I didn't want to give up my goals without trying one last time.

Only a few days into the New Year, I had travelled to France to attend a training camp with Vélo Club Annemasse and another with the professional team Gan. Despite my injuries, pro teams remained interested in signing me, and Gan, a French pro team that was sponsored by an insurance company, seemed the best fit. It employed a stable of English-speaking riders, and it had a long history in cycling.

When I arrived in France, though, everything felt off. The valley around Lac Léman was blanketed in grey cloud. The humidity settled deep into my bones. Snow lined the roads, and Christian Rumeau, the directeur who had guided me during my first two seasons in France, had been pushed out of the Vélo Club. At sixty-five, he was regarded by the club as too old to run a team. It was a misguided move and a major loss. Rumeau was more dedicated, more knowledgeable and harder-working than anyone else I'd met in the cycling world. I moved back into the apartment where I had lived on and off for almost two years, but it no longer felt like a home. I was unsettled by the memories of seasons past. The loneliness I had endured while racing overseas was more acute. I missed my friends at home and my girlfriend, Dede, a US national cyclist whom I'd met the summer before at a training camp in Colorado with Mirek and our mutual friend, the cyclist Clara Hughes. As our friendship grew through the winter Dede gave me strength as I dealt with the injuries.

In France, I realised how bitter I felt about the bad advice I'd received when I was injured. Of all the people associated with the Vélo Club, only Rumeau had truly tried to care for me, and he was no longer there. The journalists who had detailed my every move in the races in which I had performed had written only a small footnote about my injuries, and it was inaccurate. In more than six months, none of my teammates had called or written to see how I was recovering. After years with Canadian teams, I was accustomed to teammates who were friends. In Annemasse, I often felt as if we were competing against each other for results that could lead to spots on pro teams. I'm not sure that many of them really enjoyed riding. For them, it was just a pursuit that could become a job. Results and races were all that mattered. To them, I was just another rider, one of many who came and went.

The Gan training camp was both exciting and daunting. If I performed during the amateur season, they would sign me for the following year. Although I still believed I could race clean and win, I also knew the gravity of the problem and how ingrained drugs were in the culture.

The team coach was Denis Roux, who had also been the coach of the Canadian national team. Like all of us, he was progressing in his career through the ranks. Denis could be harsh and critical of those who questioned him, and supportive and thoughtful to those who obeyed. The relationship seemed to shift with each performance, good or bad. Riders either liked him or hated him. I had seen both sides.

Although Denis was giving me the possibility to race for Gan, the relationship left me uneasy, and I was concerned about his tempestuous nature. The constant ache in my back and leg also made me question whether or not I was ready to race.

The off season had been long. I'd spent three months in a metal corset, only removing it to shower and to sleep. To stay sane, to refocus my thoughts and alter my perspective, I walked through Toronto daily, from north to south and back, covering kilometres, reflecting and absorbing everything I had missed while on a bike in France. The energy expended by walking put me at peace. Being home again with my parents and old friends, I no longer felt the loneliness I'd endured in a foreign country. As I healed, I was able to move more freely. My motivation peaked the moment I was able to ride again. But the pain persisted. It nagged at me on the bike and through the night, a constant reminder of how my body had changed. I had good days and bad days. My fitness slowly returned but I lacked the ability to put out power consistently day after day. I patiently waited for its return.

The Gan training camp was a week long. In fact, it was more than a training camp. It allowed the riders to meet the staff, relationships to develop and logistics to be sorted out before the start of the season. The camp took place in January, only weeks before the season began, but the training was fairly easy. In those days, the demands of the racing calendar still allowed riders to build our fitness more gradually.

Many of the Gan riders were already my heroes. I spent a fair amount of time with Henk Vogels and often sat at the table with the other English-speaking riders like Chris Boardman, Stuart O'Grady, Magnus Backstedt, Chris Jenner and Jens Voigt. They were all friendly, especially the veterans and Australians.

On a day when no training had been scheduled, we piled into a bus and went to the top of the Col d'Aubisque, a Pyrenean peak made famous by the passage of the Tour de France. As it was still winter, the ski station was open and the snow was deep. At the summit we rented sleds and raced each other like mad children down the mountainside. Inevitably, one of the group, Chris Jenner, injured a rib. Competitive to the core, cyclists don't back off easily in any contest. Before moving down the mountain to a restaurant, we went to a bar to drink Kir Royale and toast the coming season. It was comforting to see the human side of riders whom I had idolised as they let loose, sang and drank. They dropped the masks they wore while racing, the grimaces in races, the seriousness, and the controlled messages they delivered to the media. They revealed the jovial qualities we look for in friends. To initiate the neo-pros and new recruits we each had to sing a song, standing on a chair in the dining room. I chose AC/DC's 'You Shook Me All Night

Long'. The Aussies, O'Grady and Vogels, joined in the chorus.

I was young, naive, blinded by their stardom, and fearful of what I didn't know. I wondered if the team was systematically doping its riders and if management would pressure me to dope if I joined. I felt that this was a moment I should embrace and celebrate, but it felt uncertain, far removed from my childhood dream.

After our week of training in the foothills of the Pyrenees, I returned to Annemasse and continued with my amateur teammates to a small town in the south of France called La Londe-les-Maures. We now had a mechanics' truck to store and move the bikes. We had fancy new jerseys and a roster of potent riders, although with most of them I had nothing in common. Without Rumeau, the team had lost its allure for me. In many respects Rumeau had kept me in line. He had tried to care for me, and protect me, like his son. The team had changed on every level. I didn't want to be there. Mentally and physically fragile from the trials of the last year, I found the training camp overwhelming.

As the training load increased and I accumulated kilometres, the aching in my leg increased. I had lost the power I'd acquired in previous years, but I stupidly tried to match my teammates' pace. I was afraid that my weakness would push me down the hierarchy. Having been the team leader once, I didn't want to relinquish my position.

Inevitably, the stress led to an injury. With a sore knee, back and leg, I climbed into the car midway through a training ride. The directeur took me directly to the hospital for an MRI. The next morning, I walked on the beach, collected pebbles and shells, wrote a poem on a scrap of paper as I tried to make sense of what I had committed my life to and where it would take me. I returned to Annemasse, relieved I no longer had to ride with pain.

A week later, after a battery of tests, the club management arranged a visit to a doctor in Chamonix who worked with professional athletes. He reviewed the bone images and told me that I would never become a pro bike racer because the bone had set at an angle, which would affect my biomechanics and my pedalling. He explained that I would be less powerful, increasingly uncomfortable in the saddle, and that with time the ball of my femur and pelvis would wear out as I accumulated pedal strokes. I resisted his verdict.

Another week passed and another doctor, this time an orthopedic surgeon from Grenoble, reviewed the images, tested me and questioned me, and ran another battery of scans. Gabrielle had driven me to the hospital, and as we waited for the results, we spent the afternoon visiting the town centre. As she explained some of the history of the town, I popped chocolate after chocolate in my mouth, devouring a box we had bought to bring back to Annemasse. My thoughts were drifting, nervous about the doctor's prognosis and uncertain of whose opinion I could trust. As the sun set and the air temperature dropped below freezing, we returned to the hospital for the results. The doctor explained that to race professionally my body needed to be in top condition and that, due to the fractures, my biomechanics were no longer ideal. I wouldn't be able to produce the required power to succeed. Again I wasn't willing to accept this judgement.

Not wanting to give up, I flew back to North America to be with my family, to visit Dede in Boulder, and to ride again. I rested for a while and progressively began to rebuild my strength. Once on the bike again, I disregarded my coaches' training advice and followed the guidance of my own mental and physical sensations.

Riding uphill in Estes Park in Colorado, I passed another cyclist, waved hello, and pushed harder over the top of the climb before tucking low onto my top tube for the descent into the town centre. Spring snow swirled in the air. The summer tourists had yet to invade with their motorhomes, and the town was quiet as I stopped at a small cafe to warm up, eat, and refill my pockets and bottles with food and water. Snow fell harder, but it was not yet cold enough for it to accumulate on the road. I had a choice: to go back down the mountain, shortening the ride significantly by retracing my route, or to push on higher into the mountains, as I had planned. The storm could blow through, or it could become worse as I climbed and the temperature dropped. I decided to take my chances.

As I climbed higher, the snow fell harder. I dug into my pockets and pulled on warmer gloves. Drivers cheered me, tooting out friendly honks as they passed in their pickup trucks and old jalopies. The falling snow, which now began to build up on the road, brought a new meaning to the ride as I pushed on: it was becoming an adventure and a challenge.

Close to the tree line, my tyres etched a line in the snow. The air became thinner. My effort increased, my fingertips grew colder, my face stung from the pelting snow and wind, and my shins were covered in a thin layer of ice. Fewer cars passed. The odometer on my handlebars climbed over 180 km. By the time I returned to Dede's apartment, this would be the longest ride I'd taken since I broke my back.

I followed the short descent into Nederland, a small town 2,500 metres up the mountain. I could feel the bite of the cold as it entered my core. Pedalling consistently for hours while climbing had kept me warm. But in two short kilometres of descending, I began to freeze. The descent down the canyon and back home would take me an hour. I pressed on, knowing I would arrive frozen but not wanting to give up or even stop for a moment. Racing down the canyon, I felt elated and free again.

Dede was away racing in California, and the apartment was empty. My hands were so cold, I couldn't put the key in the lock or turn the doorknob. I went across the street to a bagel shop to warm up. Then I returned to the apartment to try again. I felt better than I had in months.

Far from Europe, I had rediscovered what I had lost. The negativity that had drained my energy and distorted my dreams was gone. I no longer heard my teammates talking about which riders might be taking which drugs or how much money had been paid by whom to win such and such a race.

France had slowly drained me. I had gone there thrilled with the opportunity to pursue my dream. For a year and a half I thrived, discovering and embracing the culture, the people and the environment. It was what I had read about as I'd progressed through my French immersion school in Toronto. It was where I had always imagined I would one day live. While my foreign teammates came and left, unable to adapt to the contrasts of life in another country on another continent, I persevered. It helped that I could speak the language, and I made a handful of close friends. But, with time, the sacrifice and loneliness of the job wore on me. Although I adapted to the culture, the distance became overwhelming, especially as I dealt with the challenges of my injuries and my disillusionment. Back in North America, I felt secure.

In the apartment, warmed from the cold, I chatted on the phone with Dede and then my parents. One ride had shown me that I should try to race again.

I contacted the national team to see if there were any races I could ride. The team had entered the Tour of Willamette, in Oregon, and the national team coach, Yuri Kashirin, invited me to join him and the riders. In Oregon I stayed with Dede, who was also racing there. With each stage that I raced, I felt better. I felt like a kid again.

Denis Roux called to ask when I would return to France, as he was keen for me to perform with Annemasse so that they could justify hiring me to Gan. The Vélo Club was also eager for my return so I could contribute to their quest for results and points. Shortly after Willamette, I returned to Annemasse to fulfil my obligation to the Vélo Club and to press on.

In France, the negativity within the Vélo Club seemed worse. But perhaps my perspective had shifted during my time away. The first race I rode, the Tour du Chablais, was an important event for the team. A hard race, it followed a course close to Annemasse, with several stages in the Alps, on mountains where I had often trained. During the first few stages, my performance wasn't impressive. I wanted to go home. My teammates chattered on about the same old garbage, while my thoughts were elsewhere, back in North America with Dede and my family. The final stage was the toughest, with one long mountain pass twenty kilometres from the finish. On the climb, I was dropped from the leaders, but I kept pushing hard. Although my vision was blurred from the effort, I could see the familiar faces of supporters and friends. I saw two in particular, Gérard and Gabrielle, my landlord and his wife, standing on the mountainside, encouraging me with the effervescence of schoolkids. Over the top I surged ahead and lifted my speed for the descent. At the bottom of the mountain, I was with the leaders again. On the last small ascent before the finish, I surged ahead one last time, following two other riders. The gap grew. We were gone. Content with the accomplishment, I didn't want any more of it. I was still ready to go home. In the final hundred metres, I passed my rivals. The win was a relief.

On the podium, I gazed out at the small crowd and at the lake beyond. My only desire was to leave. My teammates celebrated near the team car. Some were jealous, others relaxed. I wanted to be alone. With a bouquet of flowers in one hand and a trophy in the other, I spoke with a few local journalists who followed the team closely and then walked across the parking lot to the team car. My teammates had already changed into their casual clothing and were in the cars, ready to go. I had no desire to return to Annemasse with them, hearing their gossip and their excuses. I didn't want to talk about racing. I didn't want to think about it. I wanted to run from it. As I reached the car, the mechanic took my bike and began loading it on the roof rack. I asked him not to bother. I would ride home.

As I pulled on my leg warmers, arm warmers, woolly hat and long-sleeved jersey, my teammates asked what I was doing. I told them I was going to ride the fifty kilometres home. They looked at me like I was mad, asking why. I took two energy bars from the box in the back of the team car, ate one, put the other in my pocket and set off. I knew the road well from training. Several times a week I had followed it from Annemasse towards Evian-les-Bains and back. But as I set off, I wasn't sure I wanted to see it again.

Team cars, loaded with bikes and riders, passed me on their way home. To each, I raised my hand and waved. On the small rolling hills my legs felt heavy with the weight of the race. It was a feeling I had missed, a sensation of accomplishment only a cyclist knows. The air temperature cooled as the spring sun set behind the Alps. I would make it home just as the sun disappeared and the young boys playing soccer all Sunday in the field down the road started walking home. I thought of the family who owned my apartment and lived upstairs. I looked forward to telling them about my victory.

As I neared the apartment and wound my way through the city streets, I became sure of one thing: change was necessary. Mentally and physically, I couldn't keep living as I was. I appreciated riding more than ever, but the environment in which I was racing was toxic.

The team had dropped off my race bag by the front door of my apartment, along with the flowers and the trophy. I didn't open the door, but picked up the flowers and clip-clopped up the concrete stairs in my cycling shoes to the second floor. I rang the bell. The aromas of a home-cooked meal wafted beyond the threshold. Gérard answered with tears in his eyes. Like most Frenchmen born in the 1930s or '40s he had grown up idolising professional cyclists. Inside the apartment, I felt welcomed by the warmth. A fire crackled in the living room. The local radio station had reported the results on the evening news. Gérard opened his arms to embrace me.

Through two seasons I had become close to this family. They had helped me through my injuries, and offered me hospitality many times. Whenever I won or placed in a race, I gave Gabrielle the bouquet. Without them both, I'm not sure I would have raced in France for as long as I did. But this time I felt different.

Gabrielle invited me for dinner, saying she had cooked my favourite meal to celebrate. She told me to hurry up and shower, as it was almost ready.

My apartment was cold and dark. I had tried to make it feel like home by putting posters on the walls and trinkets on the shelves. The kitchen table was stacked with crossword puzzles, books, drawings and my journal – a pile of ways to kill time when I wasn't on my bike. My pen and my journal became my companions. They allowed me to divulge my thoughts and emotions as I might have to a parent or a friend.

Over dinner that night, we chatted about everything but the race. Gabrielle didn't like the suffering or the injuries. The wives and mothers are always left to pick up the pieces of the broken cyclists and care for them as they recover. Like my own mother, Gabrielle had subtly encouraged me to quit and pursue something else. But she knew how hard it is to deter someone from following his passion and chasing his dreams. We finished the meal with a flan, the dessert she made for me every Sunday after a race.

Waking up the next day, I knew it was over and that I would return to North America. I went for a ride into Geneva, where I sat by the lake, bought a coffee and ate a pastry before riding back to Annemasse. From my apartment, I called my parents. Then I told Gabrielle my plan and called the Vélo Club to meet with the president and explain my decision to him. I booked a ticket home.

As children we ride and feel free, but as time passes far too many of us become absorbed into a culture that transforms our values while we remain unaware of the changes. On reflection, I thought I could place the moment when my dream shifted and blurred into something else.

At the end of my first year in Annemasse, in 1996, in the final race of the season at Lugano in Switzerland, I finished eighth at the World Championships for under-twenty-three-year-olds. I crossed the line feeling exultant and exhausted. I had been near the head of the race, with the best in the world on a demanding course. Ahead of me, four Italians had raced off in a class of their own, as if they were in a race among themselves. Their lap times were said to have been as fast as the professionals'. But such dominance by riders from a single team pointed to drug use. The fact that young amateurs were racing like veteran pros was also disconcerting. After the race, back in the hotel, Mirek congratulated me in his room. He then shrugged his shoulders and said, 'I don't know what else we can do. I don't know how you can compete with that.' Those words deflated me, and through the winter they sank deep inside me, draining much of the joy from the dream. Even at the amateur level, cycling had become a medical arms race. Unlike me, Mirek was aware of the potency of the drugs, and it seemed to affect him as much as it did the athletes. As our coach who believed in and fought for clean sport, he was at a loss. I think he felt defeated by it, or perhaps he let it defeat him as his thoughts became consumed with negativity. There was no training programme that could match the strength of the drugs.

Another of my Canadian teammates, who was also coached by Mirek, had come to the same realisation. I had raced with him since I was a young teen. While I was in Annemasse, he was racing in Switzerland with a top amateur team affiliated with an Italian pro team. National team projects brought us together, and at the World Championships we were roommates. Our experiences abroad had been similar, although I suspected that he had seen things far darker than I and had experienced the darker realities of pro cycling. After the race, we should have been celebrating like college kids at the end of the school year, elated to be done with the season and on our way home. Instead, he started crying, sobbing as I comforted him. I gave him a hug, and we held each other, feeling the emotion of a shared experience that each of us had survived in unique but comparable ways. The emotion was more complex than I've ever understood. We never spoke of it again. We simply pushed on towards another season.

The toxic environment affected us all in different ways. People told me repeatedly that a team of riders who were using EPO (the hormone erythropoietin) had beaten me at the World Championships. There were rumours that Canadian riders I had trained with and raced against were using EPO in North American races. Through the off season, I became depressed. My thoughts no longer revolved around the possibility of great performances, but around the dope that my rivals would be taking. I no longer believed in myself as I once did. Although unaware of it, I was already defeated before I started the new season.

I no longer saw the sport of cycling as I'd seen it in my dreams. I knew now that it was not played on an even field. I had become aware of the epidemic of doping. I'd learned how races were bought and sold, and I understood now that professional cycling was as much a business as it was a sport.

12

The plane landed in San Francisco. It was the first weekend of September 2001, and most of my teammates were already talking about the off season, having grown tired of training, the pressures of racing and, more than anything else, the incessant travel. Since the beginning of the season I had accumulated close to a hundred thousand air miles, most of those between cities in North America. We knew the airports like we did our neighbourhoods. The novelty of travel was gone, and like the hundreds of business people who loaded onto the planes with us, who sat patiently waiting to be called for an upgrade, and who watched others explode with aggravation because they couldn't get the seat they wanted or their bag was lost, it was all part of the job. Dressed in our unique beige-and-black logoed Team Saturn uniforms, we stood out from those in suits, our skin dark brown from the hours in the sun and our bodies a complete contrast to most of the other travellers', whose pants stressed at the seams and whose shirts tugged at the buttons. Late into the long season our clothing now hung from our bony torsos as if it was still on the hanger.

On the plane, as I often did, I had written a short note in my diary. Dede sat beside me, sipping on water, nibbling on pretzels and nuts and reading a textbook. She had retired from pro cycling a year before and was studying at university. We had been married for almost three years. Now she was joining me for what might be the last race of my career. She raced occasionally in local criteriums to make a few extra dollars to pay our expenses. After three years of racing as a professional in the United States, my salary couldn't cover her schooling, our health insurance, our mortgage and our daily expenses. We used our savings. Financially, this life was unsustainable. I had long ago decided that if I couldn't find a European professional team by the age of twenty-five I would quit and find something else to do with my life. In December, I would be twenty-five. A few US teams had already offered me contracts, but I'd turned them down. Several European squads had shown interest but had yet to make an offer. To them, I fell into a category of rider whom they could sign at the last moment, late into the autumn. I would be a neophyte on the European scene and would start at the bottom of the roster, with an entry-level salary. My agent, Bob Mionske, had been in contact with the US Postal team. He had been told that if I performed well in the San Francisco Grand Prix, they would likely offer me a contract. Bob had approached me midway through the season, at a race in Bend, Oregon, where I had done reasonably well. He handed me his business card, which I held on to for a few days before calling him. I realised that to make contacts with professional teams overseas, I needed help. Bob was already representing a few professionals who raced for US Postal. As a lawyer he could review contracts and negotiate terms; as a retired pro cyclist he understood the sport and, most importantly, had connections to team management that I didn't. He represented me for several years. He was not only an adviser but also became a good friend.

This trip was like so many other turning points in my life. In a few days I would head home to Boulder, perhaps to enrol in classes or perhaps to continue as a cyclist, pursuing the goals that had prevailed in my psyche for years: Paris–Roubaix, the

Tour de France, the Giro. To do that, I had to race well on Sunday, maybe even win.

The team staff was waiting outside the terminal to pick us up. The familiarity of this life, the routine, was starting to feel mundane, and that unsettled me. Since the spring I had felt uneasy. I had lived the life of a professional based in the United States for three years, and I had grown tired of it. While my teammates chatted, my mind was elsewhere. In my mind I had already moved on, even though I didn't know where I was going or what I would be doing. I had trained better than I had in months, focusing on the event. I hadn't raced in weeks, and I didn't know how I would perform, but I knew that my fitness was better than it had been all season. I could tell by the way I was ascending the mountains in Boulder, the way I was sprinting around the scooter while out motorpacing, the way I could never satisfy my hunger, and how well I was sleeping. The external pressures were gone. I had decided I would not race with this team for another season. Now I just had to do my best.

If I had no other options, I was ready to leave the sport. I could be happy with what I had achieved.

In the team car, riders chatted about the coming year, who had contracts and who didn't, each trying to gauge where they sat within the potential roster and whether or not they were going to be rehired. In every team I have ridden for, it has been the same: the riders always feel as if the management is being dishonest or unfair in negotiations. Perhaps because of the sacrifice involved in the job, people believe they are owed more. Too often I heard the cliché that the team is 'like a family'. I learned after a year that it was far from the truth. In sport we make sacrifices for each other and our goal. We push ourselves to inhumane extremes, but ultimately teams are businesses, often ruthless, whose survival depends on a precarious balance of victories, sponsors and image.

Although it was the inaugural race, the San Francisco Grand Prix would become one of the most important events on the US cycling calendar. It was in the heart of a major city, the course was brutally tough, and the field was one of the best assembled for any race in North America. Most importantly, Lance Armstrong would be racing with his US Postal teammates. Other Europe-based teams would be on the start line. This was an opportunity, perhaps my last, to prove that I had what it takes to race with the best.

The night before the Grand Prix, we raced in St Raphael, in a city-centre criterium. It was my first race in over a month. For an hour or so, the peloton sped around the short loops. The speed was high. I sat in the belly of the bunch, occasionally moving out of the slipstream to test my legs and work for my teammates. The pace felt easy. My legs moved fluidly, without feeling strain from the efforts. The race came down to a field sprint. I did my job for the team and coasted across the finish line, content with the effort.

After the race, we returned to the hotel by bike, a short ride under the evening sun. Riding with my teammates, two by two, as team cars whizzed by with loaded roof racks, I no longer felt I had to do a job to satisfy others, to meet standards, to impress selection coaches or to retain a contract. I just wanted to race hard, give it one last shot and see what I could produce.

The following morning, full of food, my numbers pinned on my back and my bike glistening underneath me, I rode up and down the Embarcadero. We had half an hour before the race began. I rode along the closed city roads, past spectators sipping their morning coffees as they tried to catch a glimpse of their

Tour de France hero. This was an opportunity to enjoy one last day in front of a massive crowd racing in the streets of a major city. The flutters in my stomach were not butterflies of apprehension but of possibility, the same possibility I'd felt as a boy. I was prepared to do my best, regardless of the competition. I'd finish on my hands and knees, empty.

From the start of the race, riders attacked. As the peloton ebbed and flowed with each attack, I calmly sat in the bunch near the back, out of the chaos at the front, where riders fought to hold their position, to forge ahead or to chase down others. My legs felt better than they had in months. At the back, we each held our positions without the pushing and shoving of rivalries that would ignite between leaders later in the long race. For now, we were amicable. We chatted at the back and settled into a rhythm that would last until the final hour. I rode alongside George Hincapie, Lance Armstrong's domestique de luxe. As teenagers, George and I had raced against each other in East Coast criteriums, but he didn't know me. He was now an international cycling superstar whom I had watched on television and read about in articles. I was a decent domestic professional. As riders' bikes hit or hopped over potholes, bottles jumped out of their cages, exploding when they hit the tarmac and collapsing under the wheels of other riders. A rider in front of us hit a bottle, soaking George and me with syrupy energy drink. We laughed. He said we'd be covered in stickiness for the next six hours. As he spoke, my gut told me that we would be racing each other for the victory and would soon be teammates.

The course was relentless. We repeated a circuit through the downtown core, up and down the steep climbs, which felt more like walls, fifteen times to total 210 kilometres. With each steep ascent through the city, more riders gave in, their legs becoming limp, their bodies no longer carrying them up the hill as they did on the first laps. In the finale, there were only four of us left on the front. The rest had buckled on the climbs. The four of us agreed to work together to keep ahead of the chasing teams, who were working together to catch us, and to ensure one of us won. The financial incentives for a top finish were great. Alliances in breakaways were common in cycling. Two of us were teammates, and one of the other two was already wavering on the climbs and would likely be dropped. That left George. As his team management was organising the race, and as the US stars, they were expected to win. In fact, they had to win to satisfy their sponsors. As we closed in on the finish, my teammate began to fade and asked me to slow down.

On the last climb, only a few kilometres from the finish line, George attacked. I followed. We dropped my teammate. We'd dropped the other rider several kilometres earlier. Over the top, the gap between me and George increased, and he won the race. I finished second. On the podium, as we received kisses, flowers and trophies, the US Postal team manager, Mark Gorski, shook my hand and said he would contact my agent about signing me for the following season.

The path to continue racing, to push towards the goals I had set over a decade ago, remained ahead of me. The professional culture in Europe appeared far removed from North America's. Compared to US Postal, North American professional racing seemed amateur and provincial. In the riders' movements and in the management's attitude, the team displayed an urgency and professionalism beyond any North American team. The stakes they played with were higher. I wanted to be part of it. It excited me, but it also worried me. It was what I wanted, but

I also feared the darker elements of European pro racing, and I wanted to avoid them.

The next morning, Dede and I left for the airport. I was off to Canada to participate in a ceremony to announce the World Cycling Championships in Hamilton in 2003. Dede would return to university in Boulder. In the airport, newspaper headlines exclaimed about the race. For a day, cyclists had become superstars, and US Postal was bigger than the Giants and the 49ers.

On the flight to Toronto, I wrote in my journal and tried to digest all that had happened through the season and during the race. When I arrived at my parents' house, my dad put the kettle on as I unpacked my bag in my childhood room. I took out my dirty race jersey and shorts. I had given the gloves to a small boy at the finish. Bits of clothing that would have once been cherished items, relics to be pinned on the wall, when I was a boy were now simply part of a uniform. The bedroom was the same as it had been when I left home for Annemasse five years earlier. The painting of Eddy Merckx and Felice Gimondi climbing in the Alps hung over my bed. Miniature toy cyclists, each in a professional team's jersey, formed a peloton on the window ledge. Trophies from my youth stood in neat rows like soldiers at attention on my dresser.

On the back porch, I sipped tea and told my dad about the race, about Gorski, about George and about the future. My mother arrived home from work and joined us, and I recounted it all to her.

The next morning, while I was brewing coffee, my father came home from his shop to take me to the ceremony for the Worlds. But instead of coming inside, he sat in the car in the driveway, listening to the radio. When he came in, he said a plane had crashed into the World Trade Center in New York. We turned on the radio in the kitchen and heard the news of the second plane crashing into the second tower. Under the shadow of those events of 9/11, the rest of the day unfolded.

I was scheduled to fly to Colorado the next day, but of course the flight was cancelled. I remained in Toronto for a week, wondering when I would again see Dede. When we spoke on the phone, I could hear fighter planes flying over our apartment in Boulder.

I spent time at the shop with my dad, returning to many of the routines I'd once followed as a teenager. Without a bike to train on, I rode my city bike through town, now unconcerned with my future, wondering only about the present. I prayed in the park. I prayed at home. I wrote at night, before bed, as was my custom.

That autumn, I asked a good friend for advice on whether or not I should sign the contract and commit myself to US Postal. He warned me about the dangers of the team. He said there were many rumours that they were doping. If I signed, I could get myself into a mess, he said.

13

Still groggy from the previous day's training, I lay in bed, unaware of the time. The closed shutters had turned the room into a cave of darkness. As I moved slowly out of bed, I could feel muscle damage in my legs from the intense training intervals. The apartment was empty. My roommates were away racing. Opening the bedroom door, the bright sunlight from the living room forced me to squint. I found a bag of coffee beans in the bottom drawer of the fridge and tossed it on the counter, beside the grinder. The bag felt lighter than normal. When I opened it, I understood why. Inside were vials of Geref, a type of growth hormone, and syringes of EPO. I carefully sealed up the bag and put it back in the fridge. I was shocked, but not surprised.

From our first training camp, in Austin, Texas, I'd had a hard time settling into the new team. Like being back in high school, I felt constantly judged. I wondered if I met the team's physical standards and had the personality that they wanted. Certain riders had formed a brotherhood. Cliques were evident within the group. Christian Vande Velde, Dylan Casey and George Hincapie did their best to include me, to make me feel like one of the team, but I never really did. I wonder if anybody felt truly at ease, even after years on the team. Our jobs and lives always felt precarious, no matter what we achieved. Intimidation informed the atmosphere. A rider was either with the team or against it: there was little room for compromise.

It was evident, even at the first team dinner I attended, that

Lance Armstrong's polarising character either drew riders toward him or pushed them away. In 2002, the year of my first US Postal contract, he had already won three Tours de France. There was an aura about him. People said it had settled on him long before he'd contracted cancer or won his first Tour. When he entered a room, the atmosphere became tense. Conversations became guarded, words chosen with care. Cautious about what they did and said, everybody on the team knew their jobs were on the line at every moment. Riders didn't talk to Lance like a peer but like their superior, which he was in so many ways. My conversations with him were short and our interactions few. It often seemed he was focused on something more important. From most conversations, he took what he could use and moved on, rarely giving much in return.

At our second training camp, in Javea, in the south of Spain, we were each given our suitcases of clothing. My suitcase smelled of fresh ink from the plastic bags that held each piece of my uniform. Even though it was late in the afternoon and I wouldn't ride until the morning, I pulled on the jersey, to test the size but also to see how it looked. Along with my national team jersey, my first pro jersey from Saturn and my Team Sky jersey, it's one of the few that I can remember pulling on for the first time. Seeing myself in the mirror, I felt a sense of achievement, a tinge of pride, but I felt also slightly out of place.

At the end of the camp, we received another package. After most rides, I returned to the hotel room, nursing a bottle of energy drink, and collapsed on the bed. This time, I returned to the room and found on the bed a black garbage bag stuffed like Santa's sack. I opened it, thinking we were getting more clothing. It was jammed with butterfly needles – used to simplify the mechanics of an intravenous injection – boxes of injectable medicine, pills and several different syringes. Stunned, I dumped all of the stuff onto the bed. My roommate, Benoît Joachim, who was in his fourth year with the team, was in the shower. With his towel around his waist, he came out of the bathroom and smirked when he saw the bed. I asked him what it all was.

Vitamins, sugar and amino acids.

Okay. Nothing else?

No.

What is it for?

To use at home after training.

Hmm.

I piled it all back into the bag. I had seen one of my national teammates put a tourniquet on his arm and inject himself in the vein when we were amateurs, but I had never stuck a needle in my own flesh. Holding the garbage bag, I stood still for a moment in my damp, salt-stained cycling clothing, freaked out by the prospect of it all. Like training properly, eating sensibly and representing the sponsors well, I was expected to inject myself to stay healthy and keep in shape. Our team doctor never instructed the new riders on how to use the supplements or how to stick a needle in our arms. Maybe he assumed we knew how to do it or that we would figure it out by asking those who did. I plunked the stuff with my new clothing and team gear in front of the hotel-room door. The soigneurs loaded it all into the team bus for the drive to Girona.

One of the team soigneurs, Alejandro, was a soft-spoken Galician who paid extra attention to Roberto Heras, one of the team's leaders. He doubled as a driver and took us north in the grey, boldly logoed team bus, past Barcelona to Girona, where I would settle for the racing season. I had never been on a professional team's bus before I joined US Postal. It felt luxurious. It had grey leather seats, clean carpets, an espresso machine, a fridge, toilet, shower and television. In the national team, the Vélo Club Annemasse and Saturn, my teammates and I had squeezed into cargo vans, passenger vans and team cars. Now I felt I had finally made it as a cyclist. In the bus we lounged on the sofas, slept with our legs up, showered and ate meals. Surrounded by riders whom I had watched closely on television just six months ago riding with Lance in yellow down the Champs-Elysées, I felt on top of the world, or at least the cycling world.

While I enjoyed the ride, the veteran riders complained about the age of our bus and what it didn't have. One said it had been a shuttle bus at an airport before it was gutted and styled to accommodate a team. Maybe it had. With hundreds of thousands of kilometres on the dial, it wasn't new. I learned that, like cars in a neighbourhood, buses are status symbols in the peloton. The wealthier teams have new buses, selling them off to the poorer teams when they are worn and the engines need replacing. With time, I became as jaded as my teammates, and our bus became just like all the others, part of the motorcade, a vehicle to get us from hotel to race to hotel to airport. By the end of the season I joined my teammates in wishing for a better bus and complaining about ours.

Christian joked that the interior of our bus resembled a Belgian strip club, with spot lighting, brazen blues, red striping and plush greys. Perhaps he wasn't far off. The team was run by retired Flemish bike racers, after all.

As if we were going to the start of a race, Alejandro drove the bus down the cobbled streets and into the stone *plaça* in the centre of Girona. He parked in front of the city hall, metres from the apartment. It was an audacious entrance to the sleepy tourist town in the middle of winter.

I had never been to Girona, and I had accepted Christian and Dylan's offer to live with them. It made sense, as I would be close to my American teammates. The weather was decent, the roads were ideal for cycling, and we weren't far from Barcelona airport.

For several weeks, I didn't touch the garbage bag. It sat in the corner of my room, beside an old wardrobe. Teammates fell ill a few times with a fever and diarrhoea and blamed their illness on injectable vitamins that had gone bad, making me even more concerned. Even though Christian had never spoken to me about performance-enhancing drugs, it concerned me when he told me that he was being coached by Michele Ferrari, a doctor who was known to dope athletes and who was rumoured to be working with Lance. On the second to last day of the team's first training camp in Austin, Texas, Ferrari was at a team dinner at the house of Lance's friend Jeff Garvey. I spoke with him briefly and felt uneasy in his presence, despite the fact that he was kind, well spoken and clearly intelligent.

At my first race with the team, the Tour of Valencia, held at the beginning of March, I had medicine injected into my vein for the first time. We were staying in a modern hotel in a small suburban town. We had just returned from the first stage, where I had been dropped and finished close to last. In my room, I found the team doctor, Luis García del Moral, with a bag of filled syringes, one for each of the eight riders.

Luis resembled a crazy professor in a cartoon. He was thin, jumpy, and spoke in terse broken English. He stank of nicotine. Later in my career, I was watching a track and field meet in my hotel room with my roommate when Luis walked in with the bag of syringes, pointed at the screen and said, 'I have a good one racing there,' referring to a Spanish runner in the race.

Luis's cohort, Pepe Martí, was officially the team trainer and often supplied drugs to the riders. Pepe was calm, cool-headed and unassuming. From his comments about other athletes in other sports, I concluded that he administered his potions to a stable of clients outside of cycling. He alluded to what everybody else, in every sport, was up to. In my first year, I didn't realise exactly what Pepe did with the team. He milled around at the races, sometimes driving the second team car, badly, in the caravan that followed the peloton, other times popping in for a day or two and then leaving. He sent us training programmes that I later learned were close copies of Michele Ferrari's.

After the first stage of the Tour of Valencia, nothing seemed right. Cycling no longer felt like my chosen sport and the professional peloton no longer my chosen world. Having already showered, I lay on my bed in my team tracksuit, reading a paragraph over and over, unable to focus on the page. Walking onto the bus long after the winner had crossed the line had been demoralising. My legs felt empty. My stomach was sore and cramped. I didn't feel right, but I didn't want to quit my first race with the team. The pace had been faster than anything I had experienced before, and this wasn't one of the harder races on the calendar. Maybe it was the parasite. All I could think about was going home, to North America.

Luis injected my roommate with the ease of a waiter pouring a glass of water, but also with the anxiety of a thief picking a lock. Tersely he asked me to put out my arm. Hesitant and somewhat reluctant, I asked what was in the rose-coloured liquid inside the syringe. He became irritated and made a comment about stupid Americans. It was just vitamins and amino acids, he said.

TOP: Michael riding on the back of the tandem with his mother and father in Summerland, BC, Canada, 1979.
BOTTOM: Michael trying out his new bike built by his father, Toronto, ON, Canada, Christmas Day 1981.

TOP: Michael with his father, Mike, at the Tom Simpson memorial, near the summit of Mont Ventoux, France, October 1984
BOTTOM: Michael and Mike ascending the final kilometers of Mont Ventoux, France, October 1984

TOP: Michael on the attack in his first season with the Velo Club Annemasse. Racing in the Alps was a dream come true and a step towards turning professional. Cluses, France, October 1996.
BOTTOM: Michael (*far right*) with his Velo Club Annemasse team-mates, Rumilly, Haute Savoie, France, Spring 1998.

TOP: (*left*) Accrediation from the 1993 World Championships in Perth Australia. The first time of many, that Michael raced for Canada at the World Championships. (*right*) Racing in North America with the US-based professional team, Saturn. 2001
BOTTOM: Michael racing to eighth place in the Under 23 World Championships in Lugano, Switzerland, October 1996.

Michael and Johan Bruyneel surveying the damage sustained when he was hit by a motorcycle during the 2002 Vuelta a España.

TOP: Michael, Lance Armstrong, Tom Danielson and Jason McCartney chatting before the 2005 Tour of Georgia team presentation.
BOTTOM: (*left*) Michael and George Hincapie training with the Discovery Channel Cycling Team in Solvang, California, USA, 2006
(*right*) Michael Barry and Michael Rogers training together prior to the 2007 Tour of California in Solvang, California USA.

TOP: Sean Yates and Rod Ellingworth discussing Team Sky's plans for the stage during the 2010 Tour de France.
BOTTOM: Steve Cummings, Juan Antonio Flecha, Thomas Lofkvist, Edvald Boasson Hagen, Michael Barry, Serge Pauwels and Geraint Thomas on the Champs-Élysées at the end of the 2010 Tour de France.

TOP: Michael and his sons, Liam and Ashlin just after the finish of his final race as a professional in Montreal, Canada, 2012.
BOTTOM: Michael with his father in his workshop in Toronto, Canada, August 2013.

It was intended to help us recover from the efforts of the race. The team called it 'recovery'. I trusted it wasn't banned or harmful, stretched out my arm and looked away, staring and then squinting at the print on the wall, as the needle pushed through my skin and into the vein.

Our lives in Girona felt out of synch. We were all there for one purpose: to train for the races. We rarely associated with the local Catalans, but kept to ourselves, developing our own odd rhythms built around our training sessions. Like a useless bunch of college students, we didn't cook well. Our apartments felt temporary. Everything felt temporary. I was married, but felt as if I was drifting alone, wondering where the new path would take me. Dede was thousands of miles away, in Boulder, finishing university. I would dine with Dylan, Christian or both of them most nights at Pizzeria Mozart, the Crêperia, or another local spot. George, who lived alone in an apartment just down the street, would often join us. We stood out in our American garb, the only foreigners, waiting impatiently, with cyclists' appetites, at the door for the restaurants to open at 8.30 p.m. Following the lead of my teammates, I devoted myself to the sport, but I couldn't escape from it, even momentarily, as I could at home. There was little balance. We were immersed in one another's presence, twenty-four hours a day. It was all cycling, all the time. And we had invested our lives, our friendships and everything else that we had into it.

I struggled through my first season with the team. My health wasn't great, which is often the case when I'm anxious. I started the year with a knee injury, had lousy fitness at the training camp and floundered at the Tour of Valencia, eventually quitting as a parasite sapped my energy. The team sidelined me. Then they stopped calling. Each time I was scheduled to race,

I was taken off the roster and replaced by another rider. I wondered if this was how my career would end, being on the best team in the world and never having the chance to race. My contract was for one season, so I had to perform or I was out. I worried that perhaps Valencia had been my chance and it had come and gone. I had to change something to get my snap back.

Healthy again, I travelled to Annemasse. Despite the difficult times I had experienced there as an amateur, it was the closest place to home I had in Europe. There I could stay with Gérard and Gabrielle Cheneval in their mountain farmhouse, a nurturing environment where I could sink myself into training without distraction.

During the first few months of the season, many things hadn't felt right. The spring in Girona had been damp and cold. Our apartment was messy, old and musty. Someone nicknamed it 'the dungeon'; it felt cavernous, with thick stone walls and little natural light. I had taken over Jonathan Vaughters's room after he moved into his own apartment with his wife and child. Before I unpacked my bags, I had to clean the room, sweep out the dust bunnies, wash the dirty sheets and dump the old clothing. Under the bed, I found used vials and syringes. I didn't recognise the medicine, and I didn't want to know what it was. It didn't match any of the vitamins and minerals we had been given at camp. Along with the pile of dust and dirt from under the bed, it all went into the garbage. But it surprised me that Jonathan would be so careless as to leave biohazard on the floor, even if it was only vitamin C.

There was competition between teammates. Riders gossiped constantly. Just under a dozen North Americans lived in the same foreign town, all fiercely competitive. Jealousies developed when others performed well. Those who were doping lied to those who weren't. Those who weren't doping, me included, gossiped about those who were. None were bad people. All of us just felt intense pressure to perform, from ourselves, our teammates and our management. We were insecure. It wasn't a healthy environment.

In France, I isolated myself in the mountains with the Chenevals. Hoping I still had a chance to prove myself to the team, I trained as hard as ever, but I spent the afternoons lying on the grass under the sun, picking vegetables from the garden or taking short walks in the hills. Life regained its balance. And being surrounded by people who didn't care whether I won or lost, I felt comfortable.

On a mountain pass one day, not far from the Chenevals' farmhouse, my legs started to feel as though I had the power to push and perform again. Under the low mountain clouds, I rode up and into the mist towards a ski station, which had only just closed its doors for the season. The snow on the slopes was patchy, yet still marked from the snow machines and skiers. A small Renault van stood in the huge vacant parking lot outside the shuttered lodge. It belonged to a caretaker watching over the chalet and slopes. Cow bells rang in the distance as a herd trudged across the muddy pastures. The animals craned over fences to find green grass.

Four times I rode up and down the mountain, through the switchbacks that laced up the long slope, from the spring grass and flowers at the base to the cold fresh air at the summit. Few cars passed me. Alone with my thoughts, my breath and the mountain, I felt good. On the last ascent, I pushed to my limit, until my vision became blurred and I saw stars.

'Ride until you see Jesus,' the Canadian national team coach, Walter Golebiewski, told me, moments before a time trial where he expected me to push myself as hard as I could in a race that would determine if I went to the junior World Championships. It made me laugh at the time but became one of the phrases that stuck with me through my career. I repeated it when I obliterated myself out training, or in a race. There is a moment, pushing toward my maximum, when everything begins to get blurry, sound changes and the only focus is on the effort. The moment the effort ends, regardless of whether I've won or lost, I am relieved, calm and elated.

Finally, after more than a month of training, I was sent to a race named the Four Days of Dunkirk. The name is deceiving: it was a five-day mid-level race with six stages around the Dunkirk region in northern France, and it has a rich history. Most of the stages were flat, except for the penultimate one, which was a tough hilly circuit around the coastal town of Boulogne-sur-Mer. After three days of suffering in the wind, losing time and feeling uneasy, I still felt better than I had in months. On that penultimate stage, the hardest of the race, I was at the front of the peloton, racing past slowing riders up every climb. I reached the leaders. With each lap of the hard circuit I felt better, and then I was in the breakaway, off the front, racing towards the win. With only a couple of kilometres to go I was caught by a small group and finished somewhere in the top ten. I still had hope that just maybe I could hold my spot on US Postal.

After the race, Freddy Viaene, the head soigneur, who had worked on Lance's legs through the Tour, asked me to come for a massage that night. Freddy worked with only the most talented riders, and now he wanted to work with me. The other riders joked that I had made it now. That night, Freddy told me that he'd been standing with musettes in the feed zone when he'd seen me race through with the front group. He'd assumed that the front group had lapped me and I had been dropped from the peloton. Based on my performances earlier in the season, he figured I wasn't a great bike racer. On the race radio, he had warned Dirk Demol, our directeur, that I was far behind the leaders and would be pulled from the race. But Dirk corrected him. 'No, Freddy,' he said, 'Michael's in the breakaway!'

As the season progressed, I escaped from the insular and toxic culture that surrounded the team, only to fall back into it while on the road or in Girona. I began to accept that my teammates were doping, learning with time that few were not. I could easily have found the evidence and reported them all, but I didn't. I didn't because I wanted to ride. I didn't want to alienate myself from the sport the way others had done, potentially ending my dreams. Christophe Bassons, a French cyclist, had openly spoken about the doping epidemic; after several years of abuse, in 2001, he was bullied out of the sport by his peers, deciding to quit when several rivals tried to shove him off the road into a ditch. The same happened to Filippo Simeoni, who was publicly ridiculed and scolded by Lance Armstrong and others. In France, the cycling community said that those who spoke about doping were 'pissing in the soup'. It was a phrase I heard over and over. In US Postal, the staff and riders differentiated between good and bad media. Those who wrote negatively about the team or doping weren't spoken to. There was a clear line: you were in or out, part of the culture and sport or not. It was easier to keep my mouth shut and push on.

More importantly, I didn't want to quit, not after all I'd done to get here. I had broken bones, battled loneliness, fought against my doubts and pushed myself to my physical limits. I'd gone hungry, lost weight, climbed thousand-metre mountains in freezing temperatures, thrown up at the top and ridden down again, shivering so badly I could hardly hold the handlebars. I'd ridden over twenty-five thousand kilometres a year, close to a hundred races a season, spent over two hundred days away on the road in hotels, taken bad advice from indifferent coaches and good advice from good coaches who were fired for their troubles. I was only twenty-six years old, but I'd spent over twenty of those years pursuing this dream, and now I was so close I could taste it. And I wasn't in this alone. My friends knew what I was doing, and they were counting on me to live up to their expectations of becoming a professional cyclist and riding in the Tour de France. If I quit now, I would spend the rest of my life wondering if I'd done the right thing. I didn't realise at the time that most people do that anyway.

But in the process, I slowly became part of the culture. The team, because of Lance's success, had become the biggest thing in sport. It was a thrill and a buzz, an ego boost, to be a member of something so grand. Success and adulation boosted our egos, yet life in Girona fell far short of those heights. There we fed our insecurities. We isolated ourselves and hid from most of the press on the team's orders. I soon realised that we had to remain isolated to keep from exposing our lies. Our team's path to glory had followed a trail of cheating. Our story had inspired millions, but it was based on a lie. But was US Postal doing anything differently from any other team? That was what everyone said, what we were told and began to think. Those beliefs were based on rumours that floated through the peloton, bounced around the team bus and were spoken on training rides in Girona.

In late June 2002, before the first stage of the Volta a Catalunya, a team time trial, we warmed up: eight riders lined up in a row on our stationary trainers beside the team bus, like soldiers in marching formation, each pedalling to his own rhythm, isolating himself in concentration, visualising the race, alone in his thoughts, but all doing exactly the same thing at the same cadence, with our headphones on, in a routine we knew would bring us to the start ready to ride as fast as we could in unison. Midway through the hour-long warm-up, the team doctor called each of us into the bus, like a teacher pulling a student out of the classroom. Inside the bus, a nurse wiped the sweat off my skin and the doctor plunged a needle into my arm to inject me with caffeine and sodium bicarbonate. The caffeine was to animate us and the sodium bicarbonate to counter the lactic acid that would sear our muscles during our effort. Neither substance was banned from professional cycling but both were performance-enhancing. A moment later, another rider sat down beside me, holding a bit of gauze on his arm to stop the bleeding before he resumed his position outside on the home trainer in front of the spectators. The experience seemed odd, slightly unnerving and completely foreign, yet my teammates seemed comfortable with the routine and put me slightly more at ease. Like the warm-up on the trainer and the timed consumption of sugary energy gels, the injections were all part of the process to get ready for the event.

The Spanish teams parked near our bus would be our toughest rivals during the coming week of racing. They seemed to follow the same routine. During their warm-up, they all rode with long-sleeved jerseys, even though it was scorching hot on the road. Perhaps they wore them to sweat or just to cover up the needle marks from the pre-race injections. I became used to seeing riders overdressed in warm-ups and in races. I was told they dressed that way to eliminate water, which the body retained when injected with cortisone. Even with the drugs, a few extra kilograms of water in the body would make the difference between first and fortieth in a hard hilly race.

I, too, soon learned that it was better to have sleeves covering my arms than risk the embarrassment of blood mixing with my sweat droplets and running down my arm in front of a crowd of spectators. Even though the team was injecting me, I didn't regard it as doping, since none of the substances was banned. But at the same time as I accepted the substances, I also accepted the procedure of receiving a doctor's needle in my arm. It was becoming routine. I had succumbed to groupthink.

Inside the bubble of the team and the race, everything came down to performance. Because the caffeine kept us awake, the doctor gave us sleeping pills, handing them out like sweets before we went to bed. My roommates took them to gain the precious sleep they needed to recover so they could perform the next day. They never thought about the side effects, but naively trusted the doctor. When I looked them up, I realised the harm that these medications could do. But then, watching my teammates take them, and hearing their deep breathing as they fell asleep while I lay awake, staring at the ceiling, I gave in. I accepted the doctor's nighttime sweet to get the sleep I needed to do my job.

Soon after the start of the team time trial, we were flying. We tore through towns, cohesively working together, each rider taking a forceful turn at the front in the wind before he slid to the back and into the slipstream of the line of eight before rotating through to the front again. Our solid carbon disc wheels amplified sound like a drum. They whirred and hummed as we accelerated. They cracked and popped as we shifted gears. They squealed as we braked. Our directeur followed us in the team car, blasting the horn to encourage us and to alert the fans to stay clear as we stormed through town. It felt fantastic.

After a few minutes, two riders on the team could no longer take their turn at the front, heading into the wind. Their legs had filled with lactic acid, which inhibited their power. As we rode ahead of them, we heard one of them call out, 'I can't pull through. I'm lactating.' Since none of us had energy to spare on the bike, we waited till dinner that night to laugh at his comment.

We won the time trial. On the podium we dosed ourselves and everybody close by with cava, and then rode jubilantly back to the bus for the trip to the hotel. Geoff Brown, the team mechanic and a fellow Canadian, congratulated me with pride and sincerity, for winning a ProTour race. It was something few Canadians had done. I felt like I had arrived, but I would soon feel differently.

As the Volta a Catalunya proceeded, I woke up one night to find my teammate digging into the minifridge, pulling something out, going into the bathroom, and then returning to his bed to sleep. Although he had raced professionally for years, he was new to the team and had only a one-year contract. His career hung precariously on each performance, just as it did for all of us who had yet to prove ourselves to the squad. Even Christian, who had been with the team for years, seemed nervous about his future. His biomechanics were off, affecting his progress, and his performance had been subpar. He was right to feel concerned. In the eyes of Lance Armstrong, Johan Bruyneel, our directeur sportif, and the rest of the team's management, all of us were only as good as our last race.

Annoyed and curious, I asked my roommate the next morning why he had been rummaging through the fridge at night. Nervously, he told me he was injecting himself with an amino acid, and it needed to be stored at a cold temperature. Clearly, he was lying. He had no reason to hide an amino acid. It had to have been something more potent. At our hotel the next night, I was paired with another rider.

The Volta a Catalunya was the final selection race before the Tour de France, which only added to the pressure and the competition between teammates for the final spots. On the last stage of the race, Christian was told he wouldn't be riding the Tour, as was originally planned. Outside the bus, tears rolled down his face. I only later experienced the deep disappointment of narrowly missing out on a spot in the Tour.

The Tour trumps any other event in cycling. To the public it's the greatest show in cycling and one of the greatest in sport. For North Americans especially, it quantifies a bike racer's abilities. When we're not chosen for the Tour, we feel as if we've let down our friends and supporters.

Through the season, I found my legs and my place on the team as my performance improved. In North America and with Annemasse, I had raced to win every time I'd pinned on a number. Now, as a professional in Europe, it was far more difficult to win. The pace of the peloton was higher, the speed at which we climbed was quicker and the talent pool was deeper. A European sprinter could also climb with the best in most North American races. In Europe sprinters finished far behind the climbers, even on a short climb. To deal with the change, I shifted my personal finish line. I learned to do my job, to set targets within the race. I worked hard as a domestique, devoting myself to the team's objective and goals. It was clear that if I could follow Johan's commands successfully, I might keep my job. But even then, I never felt secure. Johan rarely developed close relationships with his riders. When he walked into our hotel rooms, riders sat nervously while he peered into our suitcases, making a mental inventory of what we carried. The conversation was always tense with Johan. We knew he was judging us by our words, our physiques and our comportment. It was only a few years later, when he knew I was no longer going to be racing with the team, that I saw another side to him, a more human side that was less confident, more personable and less guarded. He told me then that a directeur should always maintain his distance from his riders.

While I abandoned my thoughts of winning, changed my focus, dug in and tried to do my job, teammates with comparable talents to mine, who had raced with me in the US, began to soar. They joined the leaders in the Tour de France and surged ahead in other races, while I suffered at the back. The shift in their performance was disturbing. Through the rumours and the gossip of others, I knew that they were doping. They had given in to what I was still resisting.

With each race, training ride and night we spent together in a foreign hotel room or our small apartment in Girona, I became closer with my teammates. They gradually became more open, but never enough to admit to what they were doing in their rooms at night or with the team doctor. That trust wasn't yet there.

In late September the team had yet to offer me a contract, but Johan called to tell me that I had been selected for the Vuelta a España. This would be my first Grand Tour. It was also a personal victory, a turning point, an opportunity and a goal achieved. With Roberto Heras, a past winner of the Vuelta and one of the best climbers in the peloton, as our team leader, we were expected to control the race to position him for the overall victory. I had heard repeatedly how much harder a three-week race would be than the shorter ones I'd ridden so far. I felt unsure of how I should prepare myself physically and mentally. At night, I wrestled with my thoughts, imagining the courses and how things would unfold. My visions were undefined and inconsistent, and I was overconfident. But before the start of the race everything still seemed possible.

I trained in Girona, sometimes with teammates and sometimes alone. According to my powermeter, my fitness was as good as it had ever been. I went to the race feeling sharp and ready.

Three days before the start of the Vuelta, we arrived at a hotel south of Valencia, on the coast of Spain, where we would stay until the race began. Once we unpacked, the doctor called us into his room, one by one, as he'd done at most races, to test our haematocrit value. He did this, I knew, to ensure that no rider on the team exceeded the legal limit imposed by the Union Cycliste Internationale, cycling's world governing body.

Although everybody passed the test, some of my teammates were nervous when further tests were administered during the race, and several of them had chemical burns on their abdomens from testosterone patches stuck to their skin. By my calculations, only three of us weren't doping.

Hundreds of rooms in our hotel were empty. Most of the summer tourists had gone home, although a few still lingered by the pool. From our hotel-room windows, they looked like black dots on a sea of empty white chaises longues. The scorching summer had yet to cool, and we spent more time indoors, in the shade of our rooms, walking the empty hallways and wasting the hours until the next meal, in front of the television, chatting, paging through magazines or reading books. Chechu, my roommate, studied a book on electrical engineering. He was one of the top bike racers in the world, but he still hoped to complete his degree, a rarity in a peloton filled with high-school dropouts. In the late morning, we trained on our time-trial bikes in a tight paceline to prepare for the first stage, a flat team time trial up and down a highway and through town. Two days before the start, I was already nervous about the race. On top of it being my first Grand Tour, as favourites to win the stage and the overall race we would attract the cameras. A technical error could cost us the race and, for me, my career. A poor performance would let down the team. Johan would be watching every pedal stroke from the team car.

14

Back at home I clicked on the television. Flies buzzed around the room, but I was too sore to get up to swat them and it was too hot in the apartment to close the windows. Every now and then they landed on my wounds. I shooed them away. Someone had told me they laid eggs in wounds. Even if it was a myth, it had me worried. I watched the race on television. I was supposed to be there, with the team, in the peloton, racing. And three days earlier I had been. I had gone from wanting nothing more than just crossing the final finish line of the three-week race in Madrid to being relieved that I no longer had to continue. In the apartment and without my teammates I felt even more alone and depressed. I had already forgotten how hard the race had been.

Even before the crash in the Vuelta, I was no longer enjoying the race. There was nothing fun or pleasant about it. Every day brought suffering, first in the guts of the peloton and then at its tail end, while I was unable to make an impact on the race. Inside the race, a rider forgets about the audience that scrutinises the details from home. The hundreds of thousands of people analyse our performance, our tactics, without having ever ridden in the middle of the bunch, without having climbed four or five mountains in a day, without having been in the wheels of a team riding a tempo so fast and with such apparent ease, their rivals start hollering obscenities and pitching their water bottles at them. I was on my physical and mental limit when I crashed, as were two of my teammates. Our race had become one of survival. But on the couch at home, with scrapes on every part of my body except my feet, I, too, become an analyst. From there the race looks easy, the riders relaxed. Even injured, part of me still wants to be back on my bike with them. I miss the team camaraderie, I miss the challenge, I miss the emotion and pushing my body to the limit in pursuit of victory. Every time I have dropped out of a race, I have felt a momentary sense of relief and then an overwhelming sense of guilt, failure and loss.

On the screen, I could see a few of the riders who had helped me to the finish line after my crash. I now felt a unique bond with them and silently cheered for them from the couch. Covered in blood, with every piece of clothing torn and shredded, I had immediately climbed back on the bike so that I could finish. I rode alongside the medical car, holding on to the door, as the race doctor patched me up as well as he could before pushing me off to pedal the final sixty kilometres to the finish. From the faces of shock the spectators made as I passed, I could tell the wounds were worse than they felt. Adrenaline, shock and the desire to get to the finish line frequently overcome pain.

I didn't have time to be angry at the motorcycle driver who had hit me. The heavy bike had pinned me to the tarmac like a wrestler to the canvas. I couldn't get up. My legs kicked and my arms twisted in a fight for freedom. I turned my head and could see the weight above. I don't recall the screams and yells but the photographers' images captured my fear. Like a claustrophobe trapped in a dark closet, the sight of the motorcycle wheel on my chest, crushing my ribs, created panic. Everything sped back up. The heat of the motorcycle, the tarmac and the baking sun felt like an inferno around me, although my torn and burned skin was still too raw to hurt. The driver inched the motorcycle off my torso, while the cameraman on the back balanced the video camera on his shoulder. It was then that I realised I had been under its wheel as they skidded to a stop.

Dazed but knowing I had to get going if I wanted to stay in the race, I got up. As I stretched out, I started to feel the pain, first in short bursts with each movement, as tatters of fabric touched open nerve endings. Johan, who was following in the team car, jumped out with the mechanic to get me going again on a spare bike. Strained with concern, his face reflected the harm my body had sustained.

As I began pedalling, I made an inventory of the damage. It was bad. I now wore a cap that Johan handed me from the car, as my helmet had been shattered. I held on to the passenger door as the mechanic changed my shoe; the sole on the other had snapped. As I settled in for the ride to the finish, I no longer felt my crucifix swinging back and forth around my neck like a metronome. I reached for it, but realised it had been torn off.

The necklace had been a gift from my mother, prior to the 1996 Olympics when I was living in Annemasse. Weeks before she had asked me how I was doing overseas, alone. It was tough, I said, but I no longer felt as alone as I had earlier in the season. I told her that on a ride in the pouring rain, when my spirits were low, I stopped at a war memorial for no reason other than to read the plaque on the monument and take a break. To gain perspective on my loneliness, I thought of the soldiers from the town I was passing through, who had spent months in trenches, fought and died. I said a short prayer and asked for guidance. One beam of sunlight shone down. I told her it was then that I realised I was not alone. To remember the moment, we chose a gold cross together.

I wanted to go back to the point where I had crashed, to find it. I'd dig around in the beige gravel for it. But then, in my delirium, I would see the necklace lying on the road that etched a smooth line in the arid countryside: a spot of silver and gold on deep black tarmac, glimmering in the sun. I knew it would be there, if I were to return. There were no spectators at the roadside to pick it up and pocket it. We had fallen in the middle of a scorching desert with no one to help us up, hear our cries or stand with mouths open as they gawked at our wounds. Beside the road, dirt and gravel slopes led to hundreds of kilometres of olive groves. But I couldn't go back. There was a finish line to cross.

Riders in our small *grupetto*, who were rivals from other teams, became my allies. With empathy they pushed me out of the corners and up the final metres of the long mountain climbs. The pressure of their hands stung against the open wounds on my back and butttocks, but I didn't complain. Every push allowed me to stay tight in the slipstream and brought me a little closer to the finish line. At our physical limits, a little push can make all the difference. The words of encouragement they spoke over my shoulder helped me to persevere.

Once a rider is no longer a factor in a race and is struggling off the back of the main peloton, he forms a truce with his rivals. They co-operate to make it to the finish within the time cut-off. That solidarity is unique in sport. On a daily basis, the riders in the *grupetto* will share water, food, clothing and effort just to make it to the finish to ride another day. We help each other to tolerate the suffering and the work. With broken bones and ripped skin, their sympathy meant the world to me.

A couple of days before I crashed, Johan had asked me to come back to fetch water for the team. I heard his voice through my radio earpiece as we ascended a small yet steep climb through olive groves. The sun was baking us in the Andalucían desert.

Even though I could feel the sweat pouring off my brow, my jersey was dry. In the arid climate, the sweat was evaporating immediately. I was suffering too much to go back to the car, fill my pockets with eight full water bottles and then find my teammates at the front of the peloton to give them out. I hadn't been near the front with my stronger teammates all day. I doubted if I could do it now. I didn't move from my spot in the bunch for fear I would never be able to regain my position. From the team car, Johan could see me at the back of the group. He called me again over the radio. This time he said he could see me at the back. I ignored him, hoping I could put off the task a little longer, until I could quickly race back on a small descent when the pressure on my legs and lungs wasn't so great. But at that moment, the slipstream of the peloton felt like a lifeline hanging from the side of a building. If I let go, I would fall out of the race and perhaps out of a job. I still hadn't signed a contract, although one had been proposed to me. If I slipped out of the draught of the peloton, I would be unable to fight another day to support my teammates, to do my job and to fulfil the goal. I didn't want to let anybody down. It was the first time the speed of the peloton made me question whether I could race professionally.

On television, Christian rode on the front, setting a hard tempo in the mountains. The route had taken them up to northern Spain, where they were no longer under sunny skies but grey clouds. Three days earlier we'd been sharing a room in Cordoba. Now sitting in our apartment, alone with the television on, felt wrong. I was jealous of him as he soared in the hills. The contrast was too great. Alone, outside of the race bubble, I was missing the stories told on the bus, missing the dinner conversations, the inside comments, tales and jokes only those within the peloton understand.

My body was seared from head to toe, open with scrapes and covered with bandages designed for burn victims. But in the sweat that beaded on my skin from the intense late summer heat, my bandages lost their adherence, and I was developing a red rash which added to the discomfort.

After the accident the doctor, Luis García del Moral, gave me a brush to clean out my wounds in the shower. I bit into a towel and rubbed the open skin. Dissatisfied with my work, he took the brush, scrubbing with force to get the gravel, dirt and debris out. I sank my teeth deep into the towel, tears rolling down my cheeks. A week before, after the first stage, Dave Zabriskie had come running to my room, telling me to come and watch as another of our teammates Antonio Cruz, received stitches in his thigh without anaesthetic. As Tony bit down on a piece of cloth, Luis pinched the wound and sewed him up as if he was an old teddy bear with a hole in his fabric. The doctor had withheld the anaesthetic because it would have hurt Tony's performance on the bike.

Now, in our apartment, the fridge was almost empty, but I didn't have the desire or energy to go shopping. On the top shelf I found a few old yogurts, our staple dessert through the season, and in the door rack a carton of milk and some eggs. In the drawer, the crumpled coffee bag still held a few of the drugs.

The crash kept playing through my head. Not only at night, when I lay awake staring at the ceiling, unable to sleep for the pain, but when I awoke in the morning. It startled me, like that dream moment when you try to stop yourself from falling. I would wake up, my underwear and shirt wet with sweat. During the day, I replayed the crash in my mind in an attempt to control what happened and to better understand it. When I had crashed, I was pushing my pedals with everything I had. I couldn't see or think clearly. Had I been more in control, more at ease, I might have been able to avoid it. At the back of the peloton, the odds of crashing increase simply because there are more riders in front to make an error: touch another rider's wheel, clip a parked car, hit a pothole, brake too hard, hit a roundabout, signpost or other piece of the road furniture that the peloton constantly snakes around. We're going at 45 kph, and we're two inches apart. That doesn't leave us a lot of time to react. If someone in front of us goes down, there's a good chance that we'll go down too.

Even months later the vision of my crash continued to haunt me. I'd think of it while riding, when I moved my shoulders in a certain way, when I passed a corner, executed a descent, passed a motorcycle. When I returned to Boulder, the images persisted. At night, I would feel the motorcycle on my chest, its tyre pressing down on me, its shocks above me, the cameraman on the back looking down at me, the driver in front of him, braking. Elvio, our Italian soigneur, had joked that he could tell from the marks on my chest that it was a 'good tyre, a Pirelli'. Neither the driver nor the television company had apologised for hitting me. No one from the race management ever reprimanded them for running over me. Even with photos of the crash that showed clearly what had happened, the driver denied it, for fear that he would lose his job. If I had been a star rider, according to another photographer who saw the crash, things might have been different. The television crew would have been fined or possibly fired. But I was a mere domestique, and the photographers were an integral part of the show.

Through the off season I trained hard to rebuild my physique for another year. But the crash had changed me, as every crash before it had done. I wondered if I could ever race again with the same fearlessness or if I could tow the peloton onward for long enough to do my job properly. I questioned whether or not the crash would slow me, mentally more than physically. I knew I would test my limits again when I returned to the peloton, but I also knew that this crash had broken me in ways that I had not yet fully realised.

I arrived at US Postal's January training camp in California in good shape. I could ride with the strongest on the toughest climbs. Yet, as I would soon discover, riders I'd beaten in camp would leave me far behind in a race. And it wasn't just me who noticed the anomaly. Roberto Heras had finished second in the Vuelta only four months before the camp. At the training camp, he would be dropped at the bottom of every major climb. How would these other riders get so fit?

In every season, some thrive while others struggle. At certain points in a rider's career, injury or illness impedes the achievement of goals that have been carefully set months in advance. Christian Vande Velde, for example, had yet to regain his comfort on the bike and couldn't produce the power or results that the team expected and paid him to achieve. Accustomed to reaching a certain level, he floundered and was told by the team that his problems were in his head. George Hincapie had a virus that had drained his energy and upset his goal to win Paris–Roubaix. On our bikes out in the countryside, we opened up and discussed our problems and our worries.

In Spain, I now lived alone in another of Jonathan Vaughters's old apartments in the centre of Girona. Jonathan had given up racing in Europe and had returned to North America to ride for a US professional team, his final transition before retiring from racing. Christian helped me move my few belongings to the apartment. Once again, Jonathan had left it in a mess, as though he'd packed his bags in haste to catch a plane. He had asked us to chuck everything he had left in the garbage. In the pockets of his Crédit Agricole team bags we found testosterone patches; in the closet dozens of used syringes and ampoules in a container. Even though I had strong suspicions of what other riders were doing, it still shocked me to be confronted by such blatant evidence of doping and to see it discarded as nonchalantly as a gum wrapper and a couple of empty pop tins.

In spite of my shock, and although I wasn't using performance-enhancing drugs myself, I justified the actions of my fellow riders to myself and others. These were my friends. In my experience, they were good people caught up in a toxic system. It was easy to rationalise. Our doctors, managers and soigneurs all helped the riders to do it. All of them viewed doping as an acceptable part of the job. Almost everything riders did was pointed towards doing the job better. Doping was just one more detail.

In Girona, North American riders lived monastic lives. We devoted ourselves to the bike. During the season few of us drank alcohol, ate sweets, stayed up late or went to the town's bars and nightclubs. None of us used social drugs. We ate, we rode, we ate, we rested, we napped, we ate again, and we slept. We focused everything we did on cycling. Our wives and girlfriends spent most of the year in North America, visiting only for a few days when studying or work allowed.

In the mornings, at ten o'clock, we met to ride. It was our daily routine to meet at the Pont de Pedra, the stone bridge in Girona. Standing in the sun, we nodded hello to the familiar faces, but rarely said more. Although we were public figures, our lives in Girona stayed private. The Catalans respected our privacy. They rarely asked for an autograph or questioned us about races, our performances in last weekend's event or where we were off to next. Over time, as tourists flocked from around the world to visit Lance Armstrong's European hometown, to ride on his training roads and to eat in the local restaurants, that changed. In the summer months, when the streets became packed with tourists, the Americans in their fun-run T-shirts and khaki shorts, flipflops and sport sunglasses recognised us and stopped us in the street.

This morning, while I was waiting for George, I looked down at the river and watched a large fish coming up to nibble on the breadcrumbs that a small boy was dropping into the water. In the ripples made by the fish as they poked at the food, I saw my reflection as I felt a hand on my shoulder.

Hey bro. You ready?

Climbing on my bike, I rode with George through the old town, down the narrow cobbled laneways, snaking our way between people who rushed between appointments or off to work. Out on the rural roads, we settled into our tempo. Uninterrupted by cars and traffic lights, our conversation became more fluid. George had yet to regain his strength and his ailment remained undiagnosed despite numerous visits to the team's doctors. He talked about dropping out of the Classics and ending his spring campaign, and instead returning to the US to get properly diagnosed and treated. The stress had marked his face in ways I hadn't seen before. He felt under pressure from the team to ensure that he could support Lance in the Tour de France. Johan was growing impatient with George's illness and absences. The team needed him to produce results to accrue valuable points for their ranking. The team doctors didn't have answers, and they continued to tell him that his problems could be mental. Knowing they were off base, George was left to find a solution on his own and return when he could perform. The team moved on. There were races to be ridden and won. Injured riders were just cogs in a wheel, and they were often easy to replace.

As we rode towards the coast, our conversation wound from topic to topic but remained rooted in cycling. Through a sleepy coastal town we spoke about drugs in cycling and on the team. The conversation became stiff. The topic made us uneasy. But George suggested that with the judicious application of EPO and testosterone I could markedly improve my own performance and be able to handle the workload. I didn't need to take risks, he said. With timely dosing there was little chance of getting caught, and I could do my job well.

The drugs would enhance performance significantly although they would not turn a mediocre rider into a Tour de France winner. They improved a rider's ability to recover from repeated hard efforts, made him stronger and increased his oxygen-carrying capacity. He would still have to exhaust himself to finish a three-week stage race, but in that group of riders whose talent and ability are roughly comparable, even the slightest edge confers an advantage, whether it's a discarded water bottle to decrease weight, a more aerodynamic posture on the bike, or a drug.

Since the crash in the previous year's Vuelta, I had already begun to consider using the performance-enhancing drugs George suggested. I even began to justify their use for the sake of my own health. Throughout the season, my blood values and my testosterone dropped with the workload. The drugs would simply replenish what I had lost. They might even have prevented my crash by giving me more control and making me less exhausted. Maybe my body wouldn't feel so worn out after races. Maybe they would give me more job security. Maybe I would be selected to ride in the Tour de France.

How do I go about it? I asked.

Just talk to the team doctors.

As we climbed away from the coastal road and into the rolling hills which would bring us back to Girona, the conversation shifted again. There were few cars on the roads. A spring drizzle began to fall.

Back in Girona, we raced each other through the old town, up the cobbled climb past the cathedral and down again to the river and the bridge where our ride began. Just before heading back to our apartments, we agreed to meet later for coffee.

Under the shower, the warm water took the chill out of my bones. The ride had been easy enough and I felt no tension. In my mind I was moving towards a line that I never believed I would cross, and I was trying to justify my next step. Cycling was what I did. I thought of myself as a cyclist. I did not want to leave the sport. Rightly or wrongly, I thought everything in my life rested on my continued pursuit of a goal.

15

George and I pedalled our new time-trial bikes along the shore-line of Lac d'Annecy, snaking our way through the rollerbladers, dog walkers and cyclists. The summer sun beat down, lifting our spirits. Every now and then we stopped to fiddle with our positions, adjusting the handlebars or saddle by a few millimetres. We had already ridden the time-trial course that we would race as part of the Dauphiné Libéré. Its starting area, where barriers were being placed along the roadside and banners were being tied down, was an extreme contrast to what I had left at home in Girona. There I had been with my family or with George and his family, outside the claustrophobic environment of bike racing. Now, it all came back, the good and the bad.

Just months earlier, George and I had both been injured in the Classics, him with a separated shoulder in Paris–Roubaix and me with broken vertebrae in the Ronde van Vlaanderen, the Tour of Flanders. Recuperating in Girona, we'd become closer. We were both new fathers. Through the spring, our infant children had been home alone with our wives, as we took risks with our health to do our jobs. I'd realised in my time with my family that if I was to continue, which I wasn't sure I would, I needed to change, for my wife, for my son, and for the sport.

In April 2006, I'd regained consciousness in a CT scan machine in a hospital in Roeselare, Belgium. Moments after opening my eyes, I was asked questions in Flemish and then, when the doctor realised I didn't understand the language, again in English. Where are you? What race were you riding? The questions were simple, but frightening when you don't know the answer. Région Wallonne, I guessed. The doctor asked if I could move my toes. I did. Good, he said. He told me that I hadn't been racing in Région Wallonne, which took place in late July, but in the Ronde van Vlaanderen, the spring Classic, in April.

My head was locked in place, held tight by a neck brace. I shut my eyes as tears welled up. I felt lost in a foreign hospital without a clue about why I was there. I looked and listened to find someone familiar, for answers. The team doctor, I later learned, was at the finish, waiting for my teammates as they raced for the podium places. The team car had left me on the roadside for the ambulance to load me up. The race went on. George had been our leader and the favourite to win. He had seen the crash and asked if he could stop to go to the hospital with me. Lying, the directeur, Dirk Demol, said he had spoken to me. He said I would be okay, and he encouraged George to keep going. Cameramen from Discovery Channel, which had taken over sponsorship of the team from US Postal, had captured the scene on video from the team car, but they'd turned their camera away when they saw me lying in a pool of blood. At the same time, Dede, who was at the race with my father and our son, Liam, received a call telling them to rush to the hospital. The caller said later that the team thought I was dead.

In the hospital, an attendant moved the gurney to another room, where a doctor could look at my wounds, clean them and decide on the next move. In the room a small television, bolted in a corner of the ceiling, showed the race. From the corner of my eye I could see it unfold, my teammates in the breakaway. The nurse explained what had happened while I was unconscious. My teammate Roger Hammond had also crashed. He, too, had been carted away in an ambulance, but to another hospital in another town along the race route. The team told his wife that their doctor couldn't stay with Roger because he had gone to the hospital with me. Another lie.

I had little interest in the race. Not knowing how badly I was hurt, I just wanted to see my wife and son. I asked for them, again and again. Tears rolling down my face stung as they touched the open wounds. I felt broken, physically and mentally. This was not how I wanted to live. In my mind, and possibly aloud, I repeated how much I hated the sport, how stupid it was, how crazy it was. I was done, I said. I would never race again. I had a life to live with my son. I wanted to race with him around the block, wrestle with him on the couch, walk to the park and do what dads do. I feared that might not happen if I continued.

The nurse told me the team had checked in to see how I was. My wife and father were on their way. When they arrived I couldn't turn my head enough to see them clearly. Dede held Liam in her arms. My father stood beside them. Their voices comforted me in the way that only someone can who will continue to love you and care, regardless of circumstance. When the neck brace was removed, I was told to stay on my back in bed. I had no idea how badly hurt I was, but I began to feel the sting of wounds and the deep ache of broken bones.

The nurses rolled the gurney to a private room that overlooked the street. With its *pavé*, bollards and planters, it looked like so many I had raced down in the past. The ominous greyness outdoors, the occasional spot of blue, the sky spotted with rolling clouds that blew in from the North Sea, all meant one thing to me: racing. I had never been in Belgium for anything other than a bike race. When the wind blew I thought of how it would affect a race. When the rain fell, I imagined we were riding between muddy fields, in a long thin line, the peloton breaking into echelons. In town centres, I imagined finish-line banners and circuits that wound their way through the streets, beside the fairs with their sketchy-looking carousels, roller coaster and games, the aroma of sausages and frites wafting across the course, swirling through the peloton. This was Flanders. This was bike racing. The grim environment made for glorious moments on the bike. Grimaces etched in mud, legs cut open, hundreds of kilometres ridden in pouring rain, podium kisses in front of the masses. These images gave cycling the allure of few other sports. A bike race brought me back to my youth, to the moment when I first felt free from the constraints of parents and teachers, when I could cruise the neighbourhood and the countryside, discovering people and places I'd never known before, excited and discovering something inside that a ride on bicycle can evoke. That was how I had imagined racing, and how I thought it should be as I lay in my bed, looking out the window.

From the television in the corner of my room I heard the familiar passionate, knowledgeable and guttural Flemish voices of the race commentators intensifying with excitement as the battle heated, halting with crashes and calmly chatting as the peloton rolled through the countryside. The riders were reaching the finale, less than an hour from the finish. Even though two of us were in hospital, our team's tactics were still playing out as planned: George was in the front with a few teammates, poised to win his first monument, a top-tier, historic one-day race.

Then one of our teammates, Leif Hoste, made the race-winning attack with the key rival, Tom Boonen, whose defeat had been the focus of our team meetings. Immediately they co-operated, forging a gap ahead of George and the others. As I watched the scenario unfold, the riders spoke for a few moments together and then with our directeur, who followed in the team car. It was apparent that a deal had been made, with George left out, his legs strong enough to win but his hands tied by shady racing tactics and backroom deals. When the race ended, Boonen, our rival, stood on the top step of the podium with my teammates on either side. George didn't smile as the photographers' shutters snapped. Money had likely determined the outcome, as it does in far too many races, merely adding to the corruption of the sport.

In the meantime, our team was slowly changing and not just in its sponsorship. Having retired the previous year for the first time, Lance Armstrong was no longer as involved as he had been when he was racing. As a result, the dynamic had changed and the ambiance had shifted. Lance knew the type of rider who would fit into the team: selfless and committed teammates who would never question the leaders, always riding for one objective. The team was built around Lance, and the objective was winning the Tour. In an effort to win more races after Lance's retirement, the team hired semi-champions – riders who had won or placed well in the bigger races, but weren't necessarily good teammates or leaders. At the beginning of the season, at the training camp in Solvang, California, the team already seemed fractured. The Spaniards who had once integrated into the group were more numerous, and they sat together at one table. The Russians sat at another, the Belgians at another; the veterans sat together, while the neo-pros floated in-between, never sitting anywhere comfortably.

The biggest change, however, was the team's approach to races. In past seasons, riders had feared Lance in the same way as a corporal fears his general. We didn't want to make an error, on the bike or speaking with the media, for fear that we would be demoted to the smaller races on the calendar or lose our jobs.

Each one of us had seen a rider make a mistake which resulted in him being sidelined and his contract not renewed. The system produced results, but it also worked because Lance won and had the personality to lead, even if it was with his iron will.

When I lived with Christian he seemed paralysed with nervousness or fear each time Michele Ferrari came to town to test the riders he was coaching. Christian was scared that after all the work he had done in training he wouldn't perform to his, or Ferrari's, expectations. He knew that his career was in the balance. The night before these visits, Christian would be in a panic, knowing he was going to be judged by Ferrari and Lance. In a race, a rider can hide in the peloton or come up with an excuse if his performance is subpar. But when Ferrari tested his riders, there was nowhere to hide. They either had it or they didn't. On a climb just outside of town, Ferrari would test his riders' lactate levels after they'd completed a series of hard efforts, with a finger-prick of blood and a small machine. He would record their power output and heart rate. Combined with their weight, he could calculate whether they were in condition to win. Ferrari wouldn't be mad if they didn't test well, but worse, he would be disappointed. Christian's fear was justified. If he didn't perform as expected, or if he showed the slightest weakness, his career would be on the line. The pressure was always on. Being a pussy wasn't tolerated.

Lance's temperament was unique, even in the fiercely competitive world of pro sports. He hated losing. Kings don't lose. They can't. To him a loss was unacceptable, and it ate at him from within. It was evident in the way he handled everything he did, especially when there were expectations.

In the Tour of Georgia, all of us were beaten by a wide margin in the individual time trial. Floyd Landis and Dave Zabriskie, two riders who had left the team the year before, had finished first and second. On the car ride from the finish to the hotel, there was obvious disappointment. We were America's team, racing on home soil, and we were beaten. It was an embarrassment.

After our massages we went to dinner. Lance was already at the table. He sat at the end, with his hat pulled low over his brow, shovelling food in his mouth. He didn't say a word. Seeing his mood, the rest of us could tell we should also keep quiet. It was more than disappointment; it was disgust. A few minutes passed, then he got up and left without saying a word. We had all failed.

The next morning we sat in the team bus, listening to Johan's plan. He mapped out the tactics and explained the course. We each had a clear role to follow so the team could execute the plan: to put Tom Danielson, a stellar climber, in position to win. After Johan finished, we each began pinning on our numbers, buckling our shoes and preparing our food for the race. Then Lance spoke. Everybody stopped as his persona commanded our attention.

Listen, he said, we got our asses kicked by two motherfuckers who left the team. This is an embarrassment. It is not going to happen again. We need to make sure of that.

His voice was clear and terse. The skin tingled on my neck. I couldn't tell if it was fear or inspiration. Nobody spoke. These weren't words from just another rider on the team, or even our leader, but from Lance. Outside the bus, dozens of cameras waited for him to exit. Different luminaries from every realm came to say hi throughout the week. People lined up daily for autographs. They waited in the hotels, at the breakfast buffet, or anywhere he just might be. Their expectations were high. And so were ours. No cyclist likes to lose. But in Lance's eyes, in his voice, in his words, you could tell that for him, a race was something much greater.

That night Tom Danielson and the team had a commanding

lead after winning the stage. The team rode very well. Lance surrounded himself with riders who would commit to the goal and who would follow the lead without ever thinking of personal success unless it was part of the team's plan. If a rider did pursue his own results, he was sidelined. It was time to find another team.

The first time I rode the Ronde in 2005, I flew to Belgium with Lance and his girlfriend, Sheryl Crow, on a private jet from Girona the night before the race. Lance was building his fitness towards the Tour. Each race was a small step forward, a progression in fitness and confidence towards the ultimate goal. He was coming to Belgium to support George. On the plane, he was quiet and spent most of his time reading the *Herald Tribune*. I chatted with Sheryl, who was inquisitive, friendly and sociable. It was my first race in a while. Another rider on the team was ill or injured. Dirk had called me the day before to ask how I was feeling and if I would like to take his place. On this team, someone was always being replaced. No roster seemed concrete until the sound of the starter's pistol.

From the start I was told to ride alongside Lance and George, protecting them from the wind, keeping them in position and ensuring they had enough food and water. When they stopped to pee, I stopped to pee. If one of them had a puncture, I was to stop with them or give them my wheel. I was there to make their race easier and to ensure they arrived in the finale having used the smallest possible amount of energy.

The first hour of the race was relentless. More than half the peloton wanted to be in the early breakaway, which would hang out in front for the day, bringing notoriety to the riders and putting them in position to help their leaders in the finale. On a rare occasion, if the peloton was disorganised in their pursuit, the breakaway might succeed in finishing ahead of everyone else. Every rider who attacked in the break hoped he might get lucky.

In the fastest, toughest moments, sitting out in the wind, doing my job to protect my teammates, I was close to my physical limit, but aware that Lance was on my wheel, I pushed on. Knowing the difficulty of the effort, George empathetically patted me on the shoulder and smiled once the speed of the peloton relented.

The race didn't go as planned. In the finale, George missed the key move. Lance chased to close the gap to the leaders, unsuccessfully. George finished a disappointing seventh. Again, an ex-teammate won, Tom Boonen, which only added to the team's frustration. Top tens were inconsequential. On this team, only total victory counted. I'd completed my job three-quarters of the way through the race, and I'd been dropped. Dirk told me to quit and return to the bus. I could no longer help the team, and it was better to save energy for future battles. From my seat on the bus, I watched the race and waited for my teammates to arrive. Lance was the first. Entering the bus, he threw his helmet in disgust, cursing and upset at the team's performance. But when he looked at me, he said, 'Good job.' I smiled and said, 'Thanks.' It was a small but meaningful gesture given the circumstances. After he showered, he left with Sheryl for the airport without saying much to the rest of the team. Clearly our best wasn't enough. We had to win.

Now, this 2006 season, without Lance, we lacked a leader and the team was floundering.

In the hospital bed, Liam poked at the bandages that covered the right side of my face. Dede said the white of my eye had turned dark red with blood. Liam had never seen me this way.

His apparent innocence comforted me. But I would later learn that he likely understood what was happening, that he could interpret our angst and our tears. As he grew older, he had little interest in riding a bicycle. When he rode, he tensed till his hands went numb. He became cautious beyond his age.

Immediately after the race, George came to see me at the hospital. Only an hour before I had seen him on the podium, receiving accolades and kisses for his third-place finish. He looked worn from the race, with dark rings under his eyes and dirt still in his ears. He sat on the side of my bed. We spoke little about the race. He was frustrated with the result. He knew he should have won. But he seemed more concerned with my health, which calmed me in a way that I had not expected. His empathy, his concern, his willingness to quit a race that he had dreamed of winning since he was a boy to come with me to the hospital comforted me in a profound way.

In the hospital, I had time to reflect. Three years before, Johan had come to Girona with our team doctor, Luis, to meet with Dave Zabriskie and me. We met outside the *gelateria* in Plaça Catalunya, in the centre of town, only a few metres from where we gathered for our training rides. Johan had driven his car with Luis from Valencia, where they both lived. As they walked towards us, Luis carried a cooler he had taken from the trunk of the car. Dave and I stood nervously, unsure of what to expect. Both Johan and Luis were intimidating. Not only were they our bosses, they were also formidable characters. Few riders on the team ever felt at ease in their presence.

They asked where we lived. Since my apartment was the closer of the two, we decided to go there. From their manner and Luis's haste, it was apparent they were in a rush to get somewhere else. Inside the apartment, Luis pulled out the needles of EPO from the cooler, explaining as he prepared them to be injected how we should use it so that we could benefit without getting caught. Dave and I looked at each other. We each asked a few questions. Dave asked about side effects he had read about, or heard about. Luis discounted them, chuckling, saying only that if we left the EPO out of the fridge for too long before injecting it we would get a high fever that we would have to ride out and not worry. It would pass. The other answers came with the same demeaning terseness we had become accustomed to from Luis. I thought that we'd be given the drugs and then have time to think about it. I hadn't anticipated being injected immediately. Within another few seconds, Luis injected me with EPO. Before he and Johan left the apartment, he put enough of the drug in my fridge to last a few months.

Before they left, Luis said that if we ever tested positive, we were on our own. The team would take no responsibility for our actions. We shouldn't let anybody know what we were doing, he said, not even family, at any cost. Then they left. The entire visit took less than twenty minutes. From that day on, the drugs consumed me in ways I had never imagined, sucking away my love of the sport. Nothing was ever the same again.

In the hospital now, I thought about that moment and what had happened in three short years. To deal with the ethical dilemma I faced while doping, I rationalised it in every way possible. Everyone was doing it. It was healthier. It restored our natural levels of hormones and haematocrit, which dropped during intense, long stage races, often to unhealthy levels. I had to dope to keep my job.

Arguably, there was a grain of truth to all of the statements. But I still knew that I was doing something very wrong. While doping I felt guilty and paranoid, but I had continued to do it, not realising until I stopped how the drugs were affecting me. Initially I didn't feel any positive physical effects of the drugs, unlike Dave who came over a day or two later, excited to say he felt stronger than ever. I attributed that to a placebo effect more than an actual physiological change. He was also tormented, like so many others who had resisted doping but had finally given in. In fact, I don't think any rider wanted to dope or enjoyed doing it. There isn't anything pleasant about consuming pills and plunging needles into veins, hiding, lying and deceiving. It's traumatic on every level.

I had expected the drugs would make me fly uphill and turn me into a champion. They didn't. I had thought the readings on my bike's powermeter, an accurate gauge of potency and performance gains, would jump exponentially. They hardly moved. Nor did my blood values fluctuate as much as I had expected. After I had used the drugs for a while, I understood that some people needed to take higher doses of EPO than others, and I was one of them. But I wasn't willing to take the risk of getting caught by increasing the doses, so my blood values never reached the heights of many of my teammates'. Some of them were sent home from races because their blood values were near the legal limit. In some riders I saw massive shifts in performances and physique, but in others the differences were barely noticeable.

Like speeding traffic on a little-policed autoroute, we were all racing above the legal limit, but some were moving dangerously fast, pushing it to the maximum and taking greater risks with their health. For all of us, the chance of being detected wasn't great. Only those who were belligerent or careless were caught by a test.

The drugs improved my physical recovery. I was more capable of handling the daily workload, especially in the longer stage races. But I lived in fear of being caught. I was paranoid that my phone was tapped, that suspicious characters outside the apartment, who were likely just tourists photographing the sites, were actually there to test or interrogate me. I stopped answering the door if I wasn't sure who it was. I didn't answer my mobile phone if I saw an unknown number displayed on the screen. I sometimes trained in blank jerseys and shorts so that I was less easily identified on the road. The team instilled this caution and fear in us. We were to trust nobody. I became aware that the facade that had been created by all of those involved was too big to fall. Lance was the biggest name in sport. Hundreds of millions of people wore the yellow rubber bracelets inspired by his heroic battle against cancer and his dominance in the Tour. Lance had eclipsed cycling.

Even though we were at the top, riding was no longer the same. The liberty I'd felt as a boy on a bike was gone. Cycling had lost its true meaning. It had become a pursuit of money, accolades and victories, all of which were now empty because I couldn't earn them honestly. In that moment of reflection, I understood what I had become and that I needed to change, not only for my future but also for my family and for the sport.

Dede came and went to and from the hospital. She and my father walked with our son around the small town. My father visited cycling monuments and war memorials, which abound in Flanders, while Dede walked through the streets with Liam visiting speciality shops where she could find dark chocolate, crunchy bread or a carefully assembled sandwich to bring back to me in the hospital. In a few days, my father's childhood mates from England would be coming across the channel to watch Gent–Wevelgem and Paris–Roubaix with him: the last of the cobbled Classics. To them, Flanders was still a place of legend, where true professional cyclists lived.

In the 1950s my father and his pals had raced in England as school boys and then as teenagers. They'd joined massive club rides in London, riding for an entire day, stopping at midday and stacking their bikes up against the hundreds already sitting outside the cafes, which were filled with starving cyclists munching on sausage and chips while trying to warm away the winter chill with a cup of tea. It was a different era, when crossing the Channel to race on the continent with other Europeans was virtually unheard of, a journey taken by only a few.

My father and his mates have a different kind of passion for sport than most cyclists do now. To me, they rode in a romantic era, with an atmosphere similar to the one my father made in our house in Toronto. As a kid I never thought of cycling solely as a sport but as an element of my daily life. Cycling was fun. A bike got me to school or to my dad's shop. All my heroes rode bikes. I dreamed of racing bikes professionally not just because of Olympic medals or professional pay cheques, but also because I thought of Europe as a mystical place where cyclists suffered to triumph.

My father has little regard for the latest piece of carbon or the next generation of equipment. He doesn't eat energy bars when he rides his bike and seldom drinks water. His love for the sport is rooted in its long dramatic history and in the beauty and simplicity of the bicycle. In Flanders, I could see that passion clearly in his eyes. His friends, too, Rhett, Jim and Mike, were all passionate fans and keen cyclists. They'd ridden together for decades. I'd once shared their view of the peloton. But now it was entirely different from mine.

After two days in the hospital, I returned to the team hotel for two more days, which allowed me a bit more time to heal before I travelled home with my family. From the hotel, I watched Gent–Wevelgem and then Paris–Roubaix. The team was flying. But the internal rivalries that had nagged us through the start of the season became apparent on the screen. Close to the finish of Paris–Roubaix, the forks on George's bike broke, and he crashed heavily on the cobbles, separating his shoulder. Hearing the crash, our teammate looked back, saw George on the ground and pushed on. Of the top riders, it seemed, no one was sticking to the plan. Everybody was going for his own result. Although we had the strongest team, we wouldn't win, but would defeat ourselves with the fractures in the group caused by jealousies.

Watching the race, I was no longer a fan who idolised the sport. I knew too much about it. I knew races were bought, sold and fixed. I knew riders doped. I knew I doped.

Cycling is a difficult way to make a living, and races have been organised to push cyclists to extremes. To cope, we look for shortcuts. Some hold on to team cars on long ascents, away from the commissaire's vigilant eye. The weight of bikes is constantly being shaved to increase speed. We pitch away our water bottles and the food in our pockets to lighten our load. Some are obsessed with weight, like Michael Rasmussen, who was also suspended for doping. Not only did he look like he'd been starving himself, he also cut the excess plastic from his shoes, demanded special frames and parts, and rarely used a radio. Helmets are carved out to increase airflow and cut down on weight, compromising their structural integrity. Every gram and every metre makes a difference in our pursuit of speed. We jump curbs, cut through parking lots and constantly look for ways to move up or legally shorten the route by even a few metres. Every cyclist in the peloton is trying to get from start to finish as fast as possible, as easily as possible. But it is never easier. The rider only moves faster. For the ones at the top, cycling is lucrative and glamorous, especially in comparison to the other options: mining, field work or a factory job.

In an interview, after his limited admission to doping, Lance Armstrong said, 'The "help" has evolved over the years, but the fact remains that our sport is damn hard. The Tour was invented as a stunt, and very tough motherfuckers have competed for a century and all looked for advantages, from hopping on trains a hundred years ago to EPO now. No generation was exempt or clean. Not Merckx's, not Hinault's, not LeMond's, not Coppi's, not Gimondi's, not Indurain's, not Anquetil's, not Bartali's, and not mine.'

The toxic culture that had developed over a century in cycling needed to change. Almost everybody profited from it, by keeping quiet when they had their suspicions, and by encouraging it. I was among them. As Lance steamrolled his way to Tour victory after Tour victory, everybody affiliated with the sport profited, even his fiercest rivals. From the governing bodies to the managers to the riders to the sponsors, we all either knew or suspected what was wrong, but few of us said or did anything, and the few who did were ostracised. Lance protected the business that he had created and the industry it fuelled, with lies, threats, bullying and arrogance. But he wasn't alone in this: few criticised his actions and most stayed silent as the juggernaut rolled on. Conversely, everybody wanted to be a part of his dynasty. Performance took precedence over ethics. Health became secondary to thrills, victories, money and fame.

Returning to Girona from Belgium in April 2006, I felt renewed. Being home, going for short walks with Dede in the sun with Liam in the stroller, I felt grounded and healed. Within weeks I was riding again, first on the home trainer, then the open road. The endorphins kicked in, and I only wanted more of it. I wanted to ride again in the mountains, to feel the test of the ascent and the thrill of the descent, although I still wasn't ready to consider racing.

George had recovered from his separated shoulder and planned on riding up to Puigcerdà, a small ski town in the high Pyrenees, to train on some longer climbs before the Dauphiné Libéré. He asked me to come along. Although it was only my fourth or fifth decent ride on the road since my crash, I agreed. Together we climbed, and as the gradient increased we split up. I didn't yet have the strength to follow his tempo.

We spoke openly about change. We learned through media reports of investigations of doping allegations against riders, many of whom we knew and trained with. The extremes they had gone to, the money they had spent, was shocking, even to us. Like an arms race where each side looks for more potent weapons, the sport had become a ludicrous battle between doctors practising a black science.

One evening, George came to my apartment in a panic. The drug testers were at his house, he had recently injected EPO into his veins, and if he were tested he would be caught. His family spent the night at our apartment, and he avoided the test. It was then he realised it was truly time to stop. He was putting his family's future in jeopardy.

Prior to the start of the Tour de France, it was announced that the sport's top riders were being investigated or had been caught for doping: Jan Ullrich, Ivan Basso, Oscar Sevilla, Francisco Mancebo, Alejandro Valverde, and many of their teammates. In Italy dozens more were suspended or under investigation. In the cycling media there was a constant feed of drug-related articles. Several riders who were implicated didn't start the Tour, and the race began under a cloud of suspicion.

In the Tour, Floyd Landis stormed to victory in the final stages, fighting back heroically from imminent defeat. It was a dramatic finish that everyone loved. It evoked all of the emotions that make cycling heart-stopping. From home, I watched intrigued. Floyd and I had signed with US Postal at the same time, with a handful of other young North American riders. Soon after joining the team he fell into the fold of Tour riders and became one of Lance's loyal domestiques and his friend. But he was also unpredictable, nonconformist and independent. Their relationship soured when Floyd realised he could make a lot more money elsewhere and even lead a team.

In 2005, Floyd left to pursue personal goals with a Swiss team sponsored by Phonak, a company that makes hearing aids. He quickly started performing well in the top races and became one of our fiercest rivals. When Lance retired at the end of 2005, the Tour became a wide open race, and Floyd was a favourite to win.

It wasn't a surprise that he won. He had the temperament and ability, and he was willing to push the limits. Even so, when he tested positive, everyone was stunned. Most of us who were involved with the sport knew he was doping, but it still came as a shock that he had been careless enough to test positive.

Overnight, Floyd went from being adored to being alone. In the hope of saving everything he still had, he denied drug use and, after persuading many people of his innocence, raised money for his so-called defence fund. He fought the charges on every level, losing each time and then threatening to tell the truth if Johan and Lance didn't rehire him to the team.

If I was to continue racing, I wanted a different life, away from this team. I wanted to rediscover what I had lost. I wanted to stop crossing ethical lines. I had never felt comfortable with the shifting of my moral compass. I wanted to feel again the untainted thrill of pure racing. And I wanted to make sure that my son would never face the same decisions as I did if he started one day to dream about riding in the Tour de France.

That autumn, I signed with Bob Stapleton. Bob had been Dede's manager when she rode with the US T-Mobile women's team. Now he had been asked to take over the men's team and to ensure they were racing clean. Understanding this was an opportunity to be a part of something new and different which could change the culture that was consuming pro cycling, I signed a contract soon after it was offered to me. It was invigorating. George joined the team a year later, after his contract with Discovery was finished, as he also wanted to be a member of a team that was committed to changing cycling and racing clean.

I naively believed the entire roster of the new team would have the same vision as Bob, George and I did. At least now, though, young riders had options. Two teams, T-Mobile and Slipstream, had publicly stated their strict anti-doping policies. Other teams, unfortunately, did not. Within the race, I would learn to set my own finish lines.

16

In 2009 we finished as a nine-man unit in the team time trial at the Giro d'Italia for High Road (what the T-Mobile team became after a sponsor change). After crossing the finish line, all nine of us freewheeled, having squeezed out the most forceful pedal strokes in the final metres of the event. As we came to a stop just before the throng of photographers, team personnel and journalists, about thirty metres from the finish, I felt a teammate's hand on my shoulder. It was Michael Rogers, a time-trial specialist who was one of the most accomplished riders in the squad.

I have never gone that fast in a TTT. That was awesome. Good job, dude.

I was still gasping for air. I nodded and, between breaths, said something like, Thanks. You too.

Michael, who was a three-time World Champion in time trials, had been the engine of the team. Since he was a boy, he has raced. He grew up in a family of cyclists and he has always been world-class. As a teenager he began racing in Italy with the Australian Institute of Sport, signed for the top professional team in the world at the time, Mapei, then married an Italian woman. For most of his career he had lived and trained in northern Italy.

With our feet on the ground, straddling our bikes, the nine of us were ushered to an area behind the podium reserved for the fastest team. Having been the first of the twenty-two teams to start, we were told to wait in the holding area, a vinyl tent with nine chairs inside, until another team beat us. Even though the conditions could become more favourable for other teams, Michael was convinced we would win. This was our third season racing together. Without hesitating, we knew each other well enough to bolster a teammate in his moment of weakness or propel him when he was strong.

The route today was up and down the Lido de Venezia, a flat island near Venice. Being the first team off, we couldn't gauge our performance using the other teams' time splits at the time checks. This worried the directeurs, but we were convinced that time checks would have made no difference to our performance. As individuals we had committed to the team and done our best. Nobody wanted to be the one who let the others down. All we had to do was wait for the other teams' results to fall into place. That was out of our control.

The team time trial is the purest team event in cycling. The teams start one by one at intervals, aiming to complete the course in the fastest time. Five riders need to cross the finish line before a team receives a result. It is as much a technical test as a physical one. The team must find and share the rhythm of a metronome, steady yet fast. Each rider takes a turn in the wind, sharing the workload while his teammates ride in line in his slipstream. He must maintain a designated speed during his effort on the front, careful not to accelerate too violently or to slow haltingly, before ticking over from the front and then moving as quickly as possible to the last position in the line to conserve energy until his next turn in the wind. Each rider must consider his teammates in his every movement.

In the tent, the soigneurs towelled us off as we sipped on energy drinks, cans of soda pop and bottles of water. Sweat continued to drip down our faces and torsos. Each rider, sitting on a plastic and steel chair, spoke with loud exuberance about the race, in English and Italian, each recounting a different vignette. There had been tentative moments that had us on edge: we had sped around a tight corner and someone had come close to touching the kerb; we had rubbed shoulders and touched bars. We congratulated each other, not always directly, sometimes talking about a rider's impressive turn on the front, in the wind, or the consistency with which one took another's place on the front. The language we spoke was our own. We had all felt the seamlessness of the team riding as one, held together by nine riders' common focus, determination and commitment. We had complete trust in each other. We sat close behind one another, with only centimetres between our front wheel and our teammate's rear wheel. We sped through roundabouts without touching our brakes, trusting nobody would make a miscalculation in trajectory or speed. Small errors, like a rider out of position, were easily corrected. But one pedal stroke too many into a corner could have caused the team to crash.

The directeurs and the mechanic in the team car that followed were the closest witnesses to the performance, but only the nine of us had felt every pedal stroke and movement the team made, good or bad. Those were ours.

In the tent, our bodies seemed to continue racing. Our hearts kept thumping hard and fast with the thrill of the race. The sensation of speed that co-operating cyclists can reach together is unparalleled.

Mark Cavendish entered the tent last, having been interviewed by a journalist after we'd completed the course. If we won, he would have the honour of wearing the race leader's pink jersey, the Maglia Rosa, as he was the first on our team to cross the finish line.

In the tent, I sat quietly for a minute or more, still reabsorbing and digesting the effort from the race. I had pushed myself harder than I might have alone. With teammates, not wanting to let them or myself down, I often reach beyond where I might in a solo event. It's also a competitive instinct: it's worse to feel incapable of doing a job and to be dropped from a team than it is to feel even the harshest pain from exertion. In the last moments of the ride, as we neared the finish line, the effort narrowed my vision of focus: everything on the periphery blurred. I focused completely on the rider in front, his brake, his rear wheel and the road. This was the way I'd ridden in races since I was a boy.

'Ride until you see Jesus,' said Walter Golebiewski when I was fifteen.

Each of us drives himself toward the finish using a different mental energy to overcome the pain in legs and lungs. Cav's mental energy comes from fury. In the finale, his personality shifts, he loses perspective and he becomes annoyed with trivialities. The energy is what drives him to win, but it also gets him in trouble. He says things he shouldn't, things he doesn't really mean, and he regrets saying them later. Now, as he entered the tent, the ambiance shifted from elation to tension. He was clearly frustrated and angry. He berated two teammates for making small mistakes midway through the race. Like Lance Armstrong, Mark expects perfection from himself, and his expectations affect the team both positively and negatively. His leadership brings a team together. He make riders feel accountable, and they raise their performance accordingly. But their temperamental personalities also alienate riders who don't follow their example. As Cav swore at his teammates, Michael cut him short. He told Cav to shut the fuck up. Now.

Then, in an Australian accent tinged with Italian, Michael repeated what he had told me after the finish. Michael speaks calmly, and the rest of us listen to him. He also commands re-spect because of his experience. He is level-headed. He said we had gone fast enough to win, that we would very likely win and that all of us had done the best we could.

Cav went quiet. As he cooled off on the hot plastic chair, he smiled and began to apologise in a calmer tone of voice. We were all accustomed to his initial outbursts. We understood that the heat of the race changed his personality. It was how he had learned to cope with the danger and intensity of a sprint finish. The mindset drove him to win, distinguished him from the rest of us and made him a champion. Internally, every champion has a demon that stokes the fire. Every champion can flick a switch and become a ruthless, driven fighter.

Several teams had finished by now, and we were still lead-ing. Instead of forcing us to wait for an hour or so in the tent, the organisers and commissaires allowed us to go back to the air-conditioned bus, where we could relax as we listened to our rivals' finishing times over the team radio.

The team time trial was only the first stage of twenty-one, and our objectives were lofty. Michael had a chance of finishing in the top three in the overall classification, and we had the team to win numerous stages.

By the time the last team finished, we knew we had won. On the podium, we embraced, spraying champagne and then dous-ing each other in it. For the next day, at least, Cav would wear the Maglia Rosa. For a moment, we were on top of the sport.

Two years after Bob Stapleton took over T-Mobile, the team had bonded in a unique way. The first year had been tumultu-ous. Several riders in the squad didn't believe in Bob's goal to have a clean team. They continued to dope, were caught and were suspended. With each positive test, we assumed the sponsors would pull out and we would be out of work, our racing careers over.

I had come to this team because I believed in its commitment to racing without performance-enhancing drugs. At our first team training camp, I had naively thought all of my new teammates shared that commitment. But it soon became clear, when I was rooming with Patrik Sinkewitz, that some might not. Each evening, Patrik spent time on the phone with his old teammates who had been caught up in doping investigations. I heard him laughing and ridiculing our team's new direction. The Europeans found Bob's American mannerisms humorous, and they ridiculed his approach. Cycling was slow to change, and many had a hard time accepting that the leadership of a top team had been assumed by an American with limited knowledge of men's pro cycling. Bob wanted to make drastic changes. He saw the sport's potential. But he initially faced resistance at every level, from the riders to the UCI (Union Cycliste Internationale).

I knew that many of our competitors, including my former teammates from US Postal and Discovery, were likely still doping, and it was confirmed by their unbelievable performances in races. But I'd hoped that at least some changes might have occurred. In interviews and articles, I wrote about the need for reform, but often I was told by former teammates and peers to keep quiet. Some professionals agreed with me and thanked me for my efforts. Others felt that I was tarnishing the image of the sport by exposing its blemishes and making them look bad. They also likely thought that I was a hypocrite. I had never admitted to my past.

In the 2007 season, a deepening divide split the peloton. Many riders, including Christian Vande Velde, David Millar,

George Hincapie, Dave Zabriskie and Jonathan Vaughters, had recognised the need for a change, and they knew it had to come from within the sport if we were to achieve real and sustainable progress. External testing solved little. We all knew that tests could be circumvented. The root of the problem lay with the teams and with the riders' acceptance of drugs. To become a cleaner sport, the culture of cycling needed to be transformed.

Our team survived long enough to finish the season, but just before Christmas 2007, at our first training camp, the sponsors pulled out. They still had contractual obligations to us, and through tough negotiating Bob managed to secure enough money from them to keep the team going. But although they continued to fund us, we didn't have a title sponsor, which we needed to make the team sustainable in the long term. Under a tight budget and with a precarious future, a bond was forged between the riders. But at the start of the new season, our jerseys didn't have a sponsor's logo.

The majority of the riders also took lower salaries so that the team could afford to race for another season, now under the name of Bob's management company, High Road. Solidarity amongst the riders led to selfless riding and a run of victories. But our futures were insecure and the relationship between the riders and management was tense as a result. In the end, many riders renewed their contracts because they felt a bond not to the organisation but to their teammates.

Cycling teams, regardless of whether they are doping or not, have to win. To remain viable, they have to produce results for their sponsors. For their team to compete without drugs, High Road's management looked for every advantage they could afford in coaching, medical expertise and bike technology. Bob even hired someone specifically to test and develop new equipment that would improve our performance. He squeezed the sponsors for more, pushing them to innovate. The companies that didn't move fast enough were dropped as sponsors. He hired a medical team he could trust to keep us healthy and winning without the use of banned substances. At first, our rivals didn't know what to make of our team. It seemed unstable. Our jerseys changed frequently as sponsors came and left. Many seemed dubious that we could win without drugs. But before long, we began to win with consistency, and riders from other teams, attracted by our performance, the cutting-edge equipment and the thought that they could also improve in this environment, wanted to sign with High Road.

A few days into the Giro, Cav lost the leader's jersey after several crashes and a fierce finale. We returned to the bus in ones and twos. I arrived long after the others, having sat up before the finale, my work done for the day. Rolf Aldag, one of our managers, stood outside the bus, stewing. Inside the bus, the riders spoke in a hush, and the atmosphere was tense. Michael took me aside. Rolf had screamed at a handful of riders, he said, for moving off instead of waiting for Mark after his crash. Drama was a part of every team, and Rolf was under so much pressure that it must have ignited his temper. Once again, Michael assumed the role of a veteran leader, tersely explaining to Rolf how committed we all were to Mark and to the team's goal. That evening Rolf apologised. And we continued to win.

Cav won stages on the flat, other teammates won in the hills. I rode on the front with one or two teammates for several hours almost daily, controlling the race and chasing down breakaways to set up our teammates for their victories. It was an unglamorous job, but one that I loved and that I took pride in, especially as Cav became the dominant sprinter in the peloton and one of the best of all time. With a leader we could count on, the team felt motivated and confident. Winning became easier, and our winning spirit became contagious. By the end of the season, few of us hadn't won races. Our team accumulated more victories than any other. But we still hadn't attracted a sponsor.

I had finally found my place in the peloton and was content with my performance. No longer did I compare myself to others, letting jealousy brew as I wondered what they were doing behind the scenes and what drugs they were taking to win. I focused instead on doing my job as well as I could. I realised that it wasn't my results that mattered most, but how I did my job and that I did it to the best of my ability.

Being on a team that was clean, I heard far less gossip about drugs. We seldom speculated about which teammates or rivals were taking what drug, for what race and when. That negativity no longer eroded the fun of the sport. We might have felt tension with management, but between most of the riders, we felt cohesion. The only teammates who sparred were the sprinters, Cav and André Greipel, and they were fighting for leadership. These two sprinters were among the best in the world, but they weren't willing to work for each other. Only rarely did the team take both of them to the same race.

In our hotel room, I showered while Michael, my roommate, ate a bowl of cereal. Two weeks into the three-week stage Giro, we had reached the point where we ate constantly, popping cookies in our mouths, munching on a handful of nuts or slurping spoonfuls of cereal. When I stepped out of the bathroom, I picked up my phone and found a list of messages and missed calls from Dede and Bob. I felt stressed. The race was wearing on me, but, more importantly, I needed to make a decision soon about extending my contract with the team. Bob had given me twenty-four hours. We were moving constantly from one stage to the next. I barely had time to communicate with my family. I asked Bob if I could hold off my decision until the race was finished. I wanted to focus on doing my job well, and I didn't want to make a life-changing decision when I felt tired and worn out. I had also received an offer from Dave Brailsford to join Team Sky. He promised the best equipment, coaches, buses, support staff and infrastructure. The team would also take a strong stance against the use of drugs.

As we often did after dinner, Michael and I went for a short stroll, although our legs were too sore and tired to go more than a block or two. We sauntered around the parking lot, looking at the team trucks and cars, which had been cleaned by the mechanics to look like new. They'd even polished the tyres. In the back of a truck, a soigneur made sandwiches. Another did the laundry. We chatted briefly about the race, then nodded and continued on our way.

Beside the hotel, we found a bench that was so uncomfortable it made us laugh as we settled our bony bums on the oddly placed planks. Kids from a local apartment complex rode around the parking lot on crummy mountain bikes with irrelevant shock absorbers, seats pointed downward and names stickered to the tubes that evoked images of knights in battle. They jumped their front wheels a few inches off the ground, pulling on their bars as if the bike was a beast. A few others stood and watched. They didn't pay as much attention to us as we did to them.

Michael and I spoke about the future of the team and the sport. We questioned our rivals' performances, as competitors always do, especially when riders appear at ease and in control as they charge ahead on the toughest terrain. In the first week and into the second, we had been the strongest team, but after the rest day, as was so often the case, the race felt faster. We could no longer follow the pace, and that made us believe our rivals were doping, which was confirmed after the race when certain urine samples tested positive and a few of the riders were suspended. It still bothered me that other riders were cheating, but not as it once did. I was content now with my ability to race at a high level without drugs. In the past, I'd worried about other riders doping. Eventually I'd worried about my own doping as well. It had eaten away at me and taken the fun out of riding. Now, on Bob's team, we laughed a lot and we performed under pressure. The negativity and jealousy I'd once felt towards other teams had gone.

Michael and I returned to our room and turned on a movie. Neither of us slept as well as we had during the first week of the race, as our bodies churned through the night to recover from the day's exertions. Stages finished in the late afternoon, and after we loaded ourselves with food, our bellies gurgled all night digesting it. Any natural rhythm that we had followed became disrupted by the intensity of the race. We stayed up late and woke up early, and felt tired all the time.

Fatigue had begun to sap our minds as much as it did our bodies. As stage races progressed and my energy levels fell, I went from reading novels to reading magazines to sitting in front of the television or mousing around the computer screen. Dede and my mother complained that our conversations on the telephone followed a similar path toward lifelessness. By the end of a race, they called just to make sure I was doing okay and to tell me how things were going at home. Too tired to read as we had done when the race began, Michael and I gazed at a screen in silence. We joked that we resembled an old married couple, but we were too tired to laugh.

The fun we had wouldn't last. The chemistry between the riders on the team was too good. It was created by positive and negative experiences that brought us together and made us successful. But more experiences would separate us again, this time for good.

17

Just before Dede and I walked our children to school, I would send a text message to David Millar: 'Biking?' Sometime I would add 'Good morning' or 'how are you?' But most of the time it was one word. He would respond, usually within minutes, with a 'yes' and a time. We went through a ping-pong exchange of one- or two-word messages until we had picked a departure time, meeting place and route. In 2008, after David had moved to Girona, this became our off-season routine.

Without a specific workout to do, we could just ride. Without looking down at our watches or cyclocomputers, we could be in the moment, hoping it would last longer. Being outdoors, in nature, away from the chaos of town life, I felt at ease. Perhaps that's why we enjoyed our off-season training rides so much. Everything was distilled down to a simple level. In the winter months, we didn't yet have to fret about the coming season, and we could spend hours looping through the countryside. There was a goal but it was far off, and I was freed from the stress of reaching it, the pressure to perform and the demand to push myself to the maximum, physically or emotionally. Unlike pre-season training camps or mid-season rides, off-season rides freed me from judgement about my fitness. No one evaluated me, and neither did I. The training was done to accumulate time in the saddle as we rebuilt our base fitness, progressively strengthening our bodies and increasing our tolerance for work so we could exert ourselves further as the season approached without risk of injury. We could ride at a conversational pace, increase speed when we desired, stop for pastries and coffees, enjoy the countryside and explore new roads and territory. Our goals were new and fresh. Although cycling was our job, we were not yet eating, breathing and living it as we did in the season. We were refreshed, coming off holidays with the family, with a renewed mindset. As the training camps approached we would miss those off-season rides, and during the season it gave us another thing to look toward.

It was on those rides that we became closer. I slowly began to understand what David had been through when he was in prison overnight, caught for doping, investigated for tax fraud and suspended from racing for two years. He, like me, had been sucked in by a culture, a passion and a desire to win more and earn more. The past haunted us both in many ways. He had come clean after he was caught, had admitted his errors and was working hard at making a positive change. On occasion, we spoke about our pasts while riding through the Catalan countryside. For both of us, those rides were therapeutic. Sometimes, we said nothing as we ascended a climb, our breath and the tick of our bikes the only noise on the tree-lined roads. Most often, though, as we cruised through the farmland, we spoke about everything other than cycling.

At the beginning of each season our rides changed, as did our relationship. Our training rides became directed towards concrete goals. We gauged every effort and archived the rides in databases for coaches to analyse. Away at races, our friendship remained but we were rivals once again. Now there was a chance we could race together.

David, who was a member of the British national team, had initially put me in contact with Dave Brailsford long before Team Sky ever rode its first race. David had been speaking often with Dave B about Sky, a super-team that Dave was building with Fran Millar, David's sister. David was likely to ride for them, and we were excited to be colleagues on a team with a budget and philosophy that could change the sport.

In 2009, on a plane that was taking us to Paris for the start of Paris–Nice, a race first run in 1933, David spoke of the team with the enthusiasm of a boy who had signed up for an exotic summer camp. It sounded appealing on many levels. David explained how they would be clean, working with the same anti-doping ethic as his current team, Garmin-Slipstream, and mine, High Road. Dave Brailsford promised a nurturing environment in which riders would receive all of the best support and equipment. If the best equipment wasn't on the market, they would make it or get it made. If nobody knew the answer to a rider's question, they would seek expert advice. It sounded ideal on every level. I signed a two-year contract for 2010–11, midway through the 2009 season. My experience with the top teams in cycling, High Road, Discovery and US Postal, was a quality they sought.

Although excited about the prospect of being a member of a new, well funded, British team, David was torn. With Jonathan Vaughters, he had helped build Garmin-Slipstream into a competitive world class squad. To him, the team was more than just a workplace as he was invested in it, it was close to his heart, and his teammates had become good friends. In April he sat down with Doug Ellis, Garmin-Slipstream's owner, in Paris and told him he'd been helping Dave and Fran in the set-up of Sky. He explained that he was considering changing teams and joining his sister and old friends from British Cycling, but part of him also wanted to stay with Garmin-Slipstream and the new friends he'd made.

In the end the decision was made for him. Sky and the team's management announced, shortly after I had agreed to race for them, that they would not include anybody on the roster who had committed past doping offences. Ironically, many of those who had signed on as riders or staff and who weren't neo-pros already had a questionable past through their associations. Under Team Sky's approach, anyone, like David Millar, who stepped forward, broke the code of silence, admitted to doping and said he'd clean up his act was punished and judged unfit to work for the team. Anyone who kept the cheating to himself was hired. Obviously, there was little incentive to tell the truth even for those who wanted to. The decision to exclude David was misguided, and so was the team's policy. Dave B had known David for years through British Cycling. Fran, his sister, played a key role in securing Sky's sponsorship and building the team. When David won the time trial World Championships in Canada and later admitted to drug use, Dave Brailsford had been the British team principal. He had been with David in Biarritz when police questioned him for doping, hauled him to prison and raided his house.

Since his suspension, David has worked hard to help clean up cycling. The lessons he learned were valuable in reforming sport and making the public more aware of the toxic practices that pervade cycling. A zero-tolerance policy for past offences does nothing but force people to hide their errors. The alternative simply raises too many unpleasant consequences. This is counterproductive. The only way to change the culture is to talk about it, to make amends and to rebuild. If we continue to hide, the cycle of drug use will continue.

During our training rides David and I often spoke about the proliferation of accepted drugs. He was adamant that all injections should be banned, whether or not they involve illegal substances. The practice was common in almost all teams, but it was one step closer to doping. The UCI recognised the issue and no longer permits injections, although it is very hard to regulate. But it isn't only injections that are a problem. Team doctors hand out painkillers to improve performance and tolerance, a practice which is so accepted, it happens almost without anyone noticing.

In a race in Switzerland, I heard the directeur asking over the race radio if anybody needed anything from the team car. One of the domestiques was at the back of the peloton collecting bottles. A young rider on the team asked the directeur for tramadol, a strong painkiller. But tramadol is something different from an over-the-counter analgesic. It is a controlled opioid that is potentially addictive and has a long list of adverse effects. Just prior to the request, the rider had agreed with the directeur that the team would organise themselves to chase down the breakaway and then lead him out for the sprint finish, because he felt good enough to win. The painkiller would make his task easier.

When I crashed and broke ribs on the second day of the Tour, de France I took tramadol to alleviate the pain. The drug made me feel slightly euphoric. It made my legs feel painless. I could push harder than normal. It was as performance-enhancing as any banned drug I had taken, but with a major difference: it was legal. After swallowing one mid-race for four days, I decided to stop, choosing instead to suffer. I feared that with the medicine I would push myself too hard and not be able to recover properly to do my job the following day or week. Long-term, I was afraid of even greater damage if I pushed beyond the threshold at which my brain told me to slow down or stop. But I soon learned that some riders took tramadol every time they raced, along with a handful of caffeinated gels to counter the drowsiness it induced.

Cortisone is another drug that is routinely abused. It can be used to treat an injury as long as the rider declares it to the governing bodies. Far too often, though, riders fake an injury to receive the medicine, which enhances performance by allowing the rider to push harder. It also helps with weight loss. Taking antidepressants to manage the workload and to lose weight is also common, as is the use of Viagra to increase blood flow to parts of the body it was not intended to enhance. Anti-doping agencies put in place a line that we weren't crossing, but riders were being given drugs to help them perform that would never have been prescribed in a clinical setting for these purposes.

On the start line, pills float around in the bottom of jersey pockets or under the elastic cuffs that hold the rider's shorts tight against his thighs. Some riders wrap them in foil to protect them from disintegrating in the moisture of sweat and rain. Others use small canisters to hold the cocktail of pills so they are ready to be taken quickly, in one gulp, before the battle to the finish begins. Through my career, I have seen many riders go back to the team car for caffeine pills, paracetamol or, on occasion, ibuprofen, both to kill the pain of an injury and to improve performance. The nonchalance with which riders ask for these pills is unsettling. On the occasions when he's there, the doctor sits in the passenger seat of a team car driven by the directeur, with a box of pills and bandages in his backpack. When the doctor isn't there, the directeur himself distributes the pills and liquid concoctions. None of these are banned substances. They are simply given out to get us through the day or to help us win.

Because I had previously used banned performance-enhancing drugs, I knew how mentally damaging they could be, especially when a doctor was approving their use and supplying them, and how easy it was to go from a pill to a banned substance. Yet many young riders who have long careers ahead of them already consume and even rely on pills. Many drugs have long- and short-term side effects and are addictive. It is questionable whether teams should be handing them out without at least alerting the riders to the potential dangers of what they are using. But principles get lost in the fast pace of bicycle racing. In a relentless cycle, going from one race to the next and on to the next, repeating a routine where the next goal is imminent, there seems to be little time to take a moment to gain perspective.

At night, the doctors would hand out sleeping pills to counter the effects of caffeine and to ensure a good night's sleep so their riders could perform the next day. On most teams I rode with, this was the practice at every race. Too often, I used them to sleep, but their potency and long list of side effects worried me. The number of riders in the peloton who were abusing them was disconcerting. Some combined them with alcohol to get a mental high before bed, and then, once it was time to sleep, to help them doze off. Riders I raced with started asking for stronger pills. At first they took them at the race. Then, unable to fall asleep without them, they began taking them at home. Because most teams have several doctors who rotate between squads through the season, nobody kept track of how many pills were being handed out to each rider. I wondered how they affected reaction times in the race, as their effect can extend into the next day. One teammate had been out later than usual with a friend before the ProTour team time trial with the Discovery Channel team, an event we were expected to win. Needing a precious few hours of sleep, he asked the friend for a sleeping pill. The friend handed him two, telling him that just one wouldn't be enough. He popped the pills. The next day on the start line, he was still sleepy and couldn't warm up properly. When we asked why, he admitted his error. In the race, he was unable to do his job and put the rest of us at risk. Cornering poorly and unable to maintain the speed of the team, he almost caused several crashes. We lost by seconds, annoyed and frustrated.

Riders also used the pills after races finished, to get high as they celebrated the end of the event. Combined with alcohol, the pills transported them to another world. The following morning, they couldn't recall their actions or conversations from the previous night.

On several teams, I talked to the doctors and coaches about my concerns, sometimes at the back of a team bus, where most confidential conversations take place. They silently nodded and seemed receptive. I often forwarded them articles on the adverse effects of the drugs that riders were given. But the drugs continued to be handed out on the buses and during the race. We were never told about the side effects, and it was seldom that a rider was denied a pill. I asked one doctor if he would ever give the pill to a patient under similar circumstances in an office setting. He said no. I asked if he was concerned about what would happen if a rider crashed and it was found he had a drug in his body which normally came with a warning that it should not be consumed while operating a vehicle. He was silent. I asked how he would feel if insurance wouldn't cover a rider who had crashed with the drug in his system. He was silent. I asked how he would feel if that rider died. Silence, again. I suggested that the team should maintain an inventory of the drugs given out at each race and pass it along to the doctor at the next race. To my knowledge, that was never done.

Immersed in our bubble, there is little or no time to slow down, to reflect on decisions. That's both good and bad. If we relent, we are out of the race. So we learn to suffer to extremes. We also trust and rely on coaches, doctors, peers and managers for advice, to aid and heal us, to help us perform. Yet all of them are biased, and they profit from our short-term productivity. Their perspectives are often even more narrow than ours. For them, our bodies are tools that they need to win the next race and justify their jobs, that they can use and then discard when we no longer win races or fulfil our job as a domestique. We are all replaceable, even the best. The record-setters are soon eclipsed by others. Few athletes, especially the young, talented ones, understand the reality.

In pro sports, too many athletes, coaches, doctors and other team personnel are short-sighted and the next victory too often takes precedence over ethics, health and family. There is a disturbing trend of dealing with problems only when they become crises that can no longer be ignored. Sometimes it happens only when an athlete dies. Riders rely on and need to be able to trust the professionals who support and surround them. We are all adults, we make our own choices, but as young athletes, in particular, we make those choices with a mentality compromised by a focus on winning at all costs. The staff who support athletes need to keep this in mind when they offer advice that could alter their lives long after they pin on their last set of race numbers.

18

During my second year with the US Postal team, my teammate Damon Kluck said, 'I feel like we're in a big bubble, and there is a pin scratching the side, you know, the pin is poking and making that squeaking noise as if it will soon burst the bubble. I just don't want to be in it when it bursts.'

Damon's comment played in my head during my years with US Postal and after. I thought about it when Johan and Dr Luis gave me EPO for the first time, when the staff handed us testosterone patches and oil at races, each time I injected myself, when Lance was racking up victories in the Tour de France, when Lance and Johan were burning bridges with former teammates, when Tyler Hamilton tested positive after the 2004 Olympics, when Floyd tested positive at the 2006 Tour de France, when Roberto Heras tested positive when he won the Vuelta a España, and especially when Floyd publicly filed his allegations against Lance and the team in May 2010. Tyler, Floyd and Roberto were no longer on the team when they were caught for using performance-enhancing drugs, but they had cheated, and they knew how the team had cheated, too. These were all clear reasons to be concerned. But the arrogance with which the team responded was even more troubling.

I had long thought that I'd escaped from the bubble after I'd stopped using performance-enhancing drugs. I had suppressed the past deep within me, trying to pretend it was no longer part of me. But the bond that we'd formed from our questionable experiences on US Postal held us together even after we left the team. The past would always be a part of our future.

It was clear: none of us ever got out of the bubble that was created around the US Postal team and Lance Armstrong. And now it was about to burst.

My life changed the day I started using the drugs. It was a decision that would haunt me long after I decided to stop using them. As a result of that decision, I have tried since to avoid or control questions. Guilty and paranoid, I have sat uncomfortably in interviews and conversations while the tension of the lie has eaten at me from within. I knew I would one day have to admit to my past errors, for my own sanity. In 2010, while staying in a coastal hotel in Italy and competing in the Giro d'Italia, my secrets and lies became public. It was then that I wrongly tried to bury them deeper.

The alarm on the mobile phone rang a lousy electronic tune. The phone's flashing lights illuminated my side of the dark, shuttered room. I turned over, still tired and aching from a hard day of racing, and poked at a key to turn off the noise and lights. The phone vibrated as messages rolled into the inbox. Over and over it buzzed. I stared at the ceiling and then closed my eyes, not wanting to wake up. My body needed another couple of hours to recover. This was always the case in a stage race. I felt as though I'd slept enough to get up and race, but never enough to feel fully rested.

This particular Giro was an endless journey of bus trips, flights and race kilometres. Even though we were only midway through the race, everyone was worn out. The race had started in Amsterdam, where the nervous peloton had splintered as we raced across windswept dykes. Few on our team didn't crash in those first two stages. Showered and bandaged straight after the finish line, we boarded a bus and then a plane for Italy.

From Piedmont, in the northwest, we made our way down the Mediterranean and across to the Adriatic. We had ridden a 256-kilometre stage in pouring cold rain and another in equally bad conditions across the gravel roads in Tuscany.

At night, I had tried to write, but I couldn't think coherently. Stage race fatigue had set in. I couldn't sleep, yet I didn't have the energy to do much other than lie in bed. My roommate, C. J. Sutton, and I had listened to music that night and made a playlist for the next day's bus ride to animate the team before the stage. Before we finally fell asleep, just after midnight, we watched part of a movie on his computer. I was tired, but I was still having fun. My fitness was good, and the team was riding well.

C.J. was still fast asleep. I gave him a nudge. He stirred. With every passing second I felt slightly more awake. I turned onto my side, picked up the phone, poked at it again and scrolled through the messages.

Across an ocean and a continent, news had broken at the Tour of California that would forever change sport. Scanning the subject lines on the emails, I realised my life would never be the same. I felt sick. My stomach churned, although it felt empty. I put down the phone. I closed my eyes. I picked it up and began reading each email. This was the moment I had foreseen. Several emails were from Dede, explaining what she had read and heard. George Hincapie, who was racing in California, knew I was asleep in Italy, and he had sent her a series of messages explaining that Floyd Landis, our former teammate with US Postal, had admitted to doping. Floyd had named us and several of our teammates as having doped with him.

At this point, Landis had no credibility with outsiders. He had battled for four years to protest his innocence, only to finally admit he had been lying all along. Only those inside the sport, who understood the culture, paid Landis much attention.

I didn't say a word to C.J. I put on my team tracksuit, walked out of the room and called Dede. She answered after one ring. Through the night, while I was in a deep sleep, she had been on the phone speaking with family and friends. In Italy, isolated within my team and in the race, I felt alone. I didn't know where to turn for help. The allegations were serious and career-ending if proven. I feared my admission would affect my current teammates and others who weren't directly involved. It would also damage the team's image and its relationship with Sky. I wanted to make everything go away. I wanted to deal with my past on my own terms, as I had been doing. Riding with David Millar, I knew how his admissions to doping had affected his life on every level. Long after he had served his suspension, he was still vilified despite making a comeback, racing clean and working to change the culture in cycling and rid the sport of doping. I worried about what my parents would think. How ashamed they would be and the embarrassment they would feel. I worried about my reputation in Canada, having seen how the nation had turned on Ben Johnson the moment he tested positive at the 1988 Olympics. In the eyes of most Canadians, he went from hero to cheat, from a revered Canadian to a Jamaican immigrant. I worried that Team Sky could pay the price for my past mistakes through loss of sponsorship and false suspicions. I was angry with Floyd for bringing me into it. He could have named dozens of riders but instead identified only a handful. I wondered if it was because I hadn't supported him and defended him when he had tested positive, whether I had upset him, or whether he didn't like that I had spoken out against drug use after leaving US Postal, when he knew I had once doped and never admitted it.

After a brief chat with Dede, I went for breakfast. I felt ill yet in control. At the table, few people knew what Floyd had said, but the entire dining room would soon start talking about it after the news spread. At the buffet, I filled my plate with my usual pre-race breakfast: a brioche and a plain omelette. Chugging a glass of juice, I walked around the room trying to find my team's table amidst the dozen others who were staying at the hotel. To supplement the often limited hotel breakfast, each team buys cereal, jam, honey, Parmesan cheese, olive oil and everything else a rider might want or need to eat before a race. The soigneurs wake up hours before the riders and pile the extra food on the table half an hour before we are scheduled to eat. There is often so much that we need to reshuffle the boxes, bottles and jars like pieces of a puzzle to fit our plates and cups on the table. Buried in the pile on each table, a little sign identifies the team that sits there. Usually, I can identify a team by its food. Teams of each nationality add slightly different products to their tables. At Team Sky, being British, we had porridge and English marmalades. Teams with smaller budgets buy less food and less expensive supermarket-branded products.

Finding my team's table at last, I spooned a bowl of porridge from the pot. I had awoken starving, as I usually do in a stage race, but now my appetite had been consumed by anxiety. I forced down bites, knowing there was still a race to ride.

As my teammates came down in pairs, as roommates, they settled into their morning feast. Several thumbed at their phones as they arrived at the table. After reading an email, or a headline, Greg Henderson looked up from his phone, put it down and said, 'Fuuuck. Did you see what Floyd said about Lance?' I nodded. They would find out soon that I was involved too, but for the moment I didn't allude to anything. They'd seen nothing about my involvement. For now, the headlines were about Lance. Within hours, though, the details would be released, and the press would start calling me.

US Postal in general and Lance in particular had been suspect since his first Tour victory, in 1999. Even now, amongst a cleaner generation of cyclists, as teams tried to enforce their own anti-doping policies, no pro cyclist was unaware of the culture of doping. Suddenly, I felt as if every rider in the dining hall was looking at me, that every conversation at every table was about Lance and us.

Anxiety dug into my chest. Even in the midst of the carnival atmosphere of the race, I felt isolated with my fears. The hotel buzzed with activity. Soigneurs hastened through the lobby, hauling coolers and bags to the team trucks outside. In the parking areas, mechanics attached bikes to the racks of the team cars and stuck stickers on the rear windows that designated their positions in the caravan behind the peloton. Their friendly greetings contrasted with everything in my head. Life was going on, the routine continued, but for me, everything had changed. I felt as though I was in a dream. Everything seemed so temporary. Yet, at least for the moment, I still had a job to do.

In the hotel lobby Danilo Di Luca chatted with journalists. He was serving a suspension after doping to win the 2009 Giro, yet he was at the race and was still accepted within our world. Everybody seemed to understand. Many had been in the same position; others were fortunate they hadn't been caught.

Cyclists like Di Luca would have been vilified in some northern European countries or in North America. In Italy, he was regarded as unlucky. Up and down the Italian peninsula, I often saw Di Luca's name painted on mountain passes and stone walls lining the road, even though he wasn't racing. I saw the names of Ivan Basso and Fausto Coppi as well. All three had won the Giro. All three were Italian icons. All three had doped, but the Italian public seemed to regard the culture of cycling as secondary to their heroes' performances. To the fans, the *tifosi*, they had simply been unlucky to get found out.

In Spain, when people asked what I did for a living, they often said, 'That is the hardest sport.' Often doping would come up in the conversation. No one asked whether or not I doped to race, but more often than not people simply assumed that I did. Most people thought it was impossible to race over all those mountains for three weeks without medicine. During the years with US Postal and Discovery, when I raced with drugs, I simply nodded at their statement and then shift to another topic. But when I stopped doping, I disagreed with that assumption. I said riders did race without drugs over mountains. I said riders could excel without doping. I defended the sport and the advances it had made.

Yet the culture of the sport hadn't changed in years. Even when a team car full of medicine was pulled over at the Belgian border on the way to the Tour de France in 1998, when the cycling world was forced to speak publicly about drug use, nothing really changed. The testing was improved and restrictions were imposed, but riders, doctors and managers simply turned to less detectable drugs and more advanced methods.

Like so many other sports, cycling confronts problems in a way that will not compromise the image of the sport or disrupt the flow of money. The athlete's performance generates revenue. His health is secondary. As long as the athlete and the sport achieve results that the public wants to see, the show goes on.

I sat uneasily on the team bus, pinning on my numbers and wondering what my teammates were thinking. For all I knew, this might be the last set of numbers I ever pinned to a jersey. I was now outside the bubble. The music that played on the bus, the music that usually animated us before the start, the music that I would sing to, became nothing but background noise. My teammates' conversations were chatter. The seams that held my life together felt as if they were unravelling. My past, which I had sewn up nicely to hide the truth, was becoming evident. I didn't know who to talk to. I didn't know who to trust or where to get advice. I wanted to be on my bike, in the race, going, focusing, riding. On the team bus, I felt detached, anxious, confused and scared. My career, my future, my reputation all hung in the balance.

At the start of the stage, I looked for Matt White, the Garmin directeur sportif. I had raced and roomed with him on US Postal and we had become good friends. Floyd had named him in the allegations. Floyd said we'd shared EPO at a training camp in the mountains. I had shared EPO with Floyd, but on another occasion, not at the camp. It didn't matter. We had all tested our blood values on Floyd's portable machine to see if our haemoglobin levels had increased, a sign the EPO was working. I remembered Floyd's anxiety and annoyance with Johan, who had expected him to win the Vuelta a España, a few weeks away. Floyd's blood values hadn't been high enough to climb with his toughest rivals, and his iron levels were too low to get the boost he needed from the EPO.

In the mess of cars, riders and crowds of spectators in the Giro start area, I couldn't find Whitey. The emcee introduced the riders as they signed the official start list on the podium. As we lined up to sign in, I listened to my rivals as they joked and laughed. Some had interesting tattoos. In the peloton, the increase in ink on skin was noticeable. Many carried a level of irony: 'Get rich or die tryin", 'Only god can judge me.' Some quotes were misspelled. Hip-hop braggadocio infiltrated the peloton; as contrasting as that culture is, riders tried to find motivation and confidence in its lyrics and images. Like badges of merit, some riders had good-luck charms tattooed in a hope that they would be protected, or perhaps, helped along in their pursuit of victory. Roman numerals marked the dates of momentous wins. Others had Olympic bands inked on ankles or shoulders. Children's names and initials were marked on torsos, arms and hands, to motivate, or perhaps so as not to be forgotten while on the road for months, if that is even possible.

The crowd cheered as the local heroes and the Italian superstars stepped onto the podium. I signed on, nodded hellos, signed some autographs but said few words.

With fifteen minutes left until the race started, I rode down the street, through the town, alone. I gazed down at my shoes turning the pedals, the cranks, the chain and wheels. I looked up at the road ahead. I took a deep breath, feeling my lungs expand against the straps of my shorts, tugging at my jersey and pulling the cables of my race radio. Exhaling, everything settled into place. I wanted to keep going, away from the race, the team, the media and my past. A short prayer buried my fears. Looking at the time on my powermeter, I did a U-turn in the road and headed back. The start was imminent. I had obligations to perform. I couldn't ride away. I didn't want to.

In the start area, nobody asked any questions. I sank into my world, ready to race. On my bike, I could release the angst by pressing it into my pedals and focusing my thoughts on the job.

The starter's pistol fired and we were off for another day. As always, during the first hour we raced at a furious speed as riders attacked the peloton to forge a gap and create a breakaway.

On a day when a sprint was likely, the breakaway riders had no chance of winning or placing, but being in the break put their team at a tactical advantage, since they wouldn't have to chase. More importantly, while in the breakaway, the cameras would focus for hours on their jerseys, drawing the attention of spectators around the world to their sponsors' logos. I had no desire to get into a breakaway, but followed a few attacks of our key rivals, neutralising the tactical game and doing my job.

Just about an hour into the race, almost as if we were following a script, the peloton suddenly stopped following and chasing an attack. We gave up; the breakaway was gone. A handful of riders with no chance of winning the stage or the classification were away together. As we slowed, they continued to push on until they became dots in the distance and finally disappeared. The moment the break forges a gap there is a sense of relief within the peloton as the suffering temporarily ceases. It was our first and perhaps last easy moment in the stage: riders stopped to pee at the roadside, some went back to get water bottles, while others peeled off layers of clothing. Like workmen going on a coffee break, we could relax and chat until a team decided to take up the chase. Then we were back to work, following the wheels, sprinting out of corners and racing up hills. How long the easier pace lasts is unpredictable and depends on several tactical variables: sometimes minutes, sometimes an hour.

As I rode through the caravan behind the slowly moving peloton, I stopped at Whitey's team car. He rolled down his window. We chatted briefly, unable to say too much in front of the mechanic in the back seat. We agreed to chat after the race. News was now breaking around the world; directeurs from every team were learning what Floyd had said.

Whitey's face showed his concern and fear. I had roomed

with him in many races for two seasons. We had become close friends. His focus wasn't on the race, but on the past and the future.

Up the line of cars, I stopped at our team car for a bottle. Sean Yates rolled down the window. 'Did you hear Floyd's named you?' he said, as I put a bottle in my cage and another in my pocket to give to a teammate. I nodded. Sean had been my directeur with US Postal as well. Although we had never spoken about what had happened in the past, I didn't think he was naive. I wondered what he was thinking, and if he would end up being involved as well. Floating in the peloton and caravan I saw several faces who had been affiliated with the team and Lance. What were they thinking? Were they scared of what was to come?

As we rode along at a steady speed in the peloton, it was apparent every rider knew what Floyd had said. The news would have flowed through the directeurs' mobile phones, over the team radios and into the peloton. The television commentators who were following the race would be discussing the allegations. Although I was in the middle of it all, I felt alone on my bike with my thoughts, as if everyone was looking at me, speaking about me, yet not talking to me. I rode alone in the belly of the peloton.

As I crossed the finish line, I kept my head down and didn't stop to grab a drink from the soigneur with my teammates in the scrum of journalists, photographers and staff. Instead, I kept going and looked for the Sky beacon, a flashing light on a pole that soared above the bus, making it easier to find in the sea of spectators and parked vehicles.

Often it has been after the race that I have learned of breaking news that has changed our world or the world. A team doctor or soigneur who has been on the bus all day, watching the race from the roadside, eating lunch in a restaurant and then watching the finale on the bus television, will be the first to tell us: the levees have broken after Hurricane Katrina hit New Orleans, or terrorists have set off bombs in Madrid. It was after a stage in the Sachsen Tour in Germany that I learned Floyd had virtually won the 2006 Tour de France with an inconceivable performance in the Alps. Nino, the team doctor, had told me. There was a sense of shock as Floyd had come back from assumed defeat to win the Tour. We all knew he was doping, but so was almost every other rider. Even so, his performance was remarkable and reflected his tempestuous personality. I never imagined he would get caught, but I wouldn't have bet against it either, as I knew he was less risk-averse than most.

Our names were now headlines. I hoped to isolate myself in the bus. Inside, I could escape questions and use my phone to find out what had transpired while I was racing. But I also knew the team management, Dave Brailsford and Shane Sutton, would interrogate me there. Brian Nygaard, our PR officer, had been through it all before when he worked with Bjarne Riis, a Tour winner who had admitted to doping, on Team CSC. I saw him as an ally who could help me, despite not yet knowing how he would react.

It wasn't the opinions of my teammates or those of my rivals I was scared of. The questions from outsiders were what worried me. Few people within cycling had ever directly asked me if I had doped.

As I entered the bus, the driver and soigneur said nothing, but continued with their post-race routine. They knew what was going on, but also seemed to understand and respect my privacy and position. Still in my cycling clothing, I sat on the bus and read through dozens of emails, some from journalists, others from friends and family. I hadn't yet spoken with my parents. My mother was walking the Camino de Santiago with friends and was out of contact. My father was in Toronto, working in his bike shop. While I was racing, Dede had spoken with him. He had asked her to tell me to call as soon as I finished today's stage. I read the subject headings in the rest of the emails. Sinking lower in my seat, I pulled off my jersey and gazed out the window and looked at everything beyond the race circus where life went on: a woman hanging laundry on her apartment balcony, a farmer working in a field, the wide open countryside and Adriatic.

Under the shower, I cried.

Clean and dressed in matching tracksuits, my teammates dug into bowls of rice as the bus snaked through the maze of cars, barriers and buses and on to the hotel. Having again lost my appetite, I picked at my rice, trying to force down whatever I could. Dave B asked me to the back of the bus, where he was sitting with Shane and Sean. As I arrived they left for the front. I was alone with Dave. The tension was evident on his face: calculating, serious and almost expressionless. There was no anger, but sympathy and pragmatism.

Dave explained the circumstances, making it clear that he would have to fire me immediately if I admitted to doping, as it was team policy. This I already knew. I had to deal with the situation on my own and I didn't have much time. My mobile phone was still buzzing with incoming emails and calls, of which I had yet to answer any. By the end of the night, I would have to do something. Everything was in the balance and a decision had to be made within hours.

If I admitted to doping, my admission would put the team in danger of losing its sponsors. It could affect dozens of people's lives. If I denied having doped, I would still have a job, and so would my teammates and everyone else. That's how I rationalised my decision. At this point, there was no evidence against the rest of the US Postal riders, including me. It would be our word against Floyd's. But to keep my job, I would have to say Floyd was lying.

Lance had already denied the allegations. He had raced under a cloud of suspicion throughout most of his career. Teammates had already claimed he had doped, allegations he vehemently rebutted. Each battle he had won, keeping his public image intact. He had also threatened, attacked and sued anyone who accused him of doping, and he would do it again to Floyd. His millions of fans wanted too badly to have faith in him. He was a godlike figure to many. But this time it seemed different. Too many of us were now involved. The pin was pushing too hard against the side of the bubble. When we were racing together, Floyd threatened he would speak the truth about Lance, Johan and the team. But he held on to the knowledge as long as he had a job and was making money, as he, like the rest of us, had too much to lose.

Discredited as Floyd had become, it would take only one or two teammates to back up his allegations and he would become a credible witness. Who would be the first to speak the truth? The rest of us had been living the *omertà*, trying to save our careers and cover up the past.

It was eating at me, the toxicity of the experiences, the lies and the culture of the US Postal team and the peloton, forever festering. My feelings weren't unique. David Millar had spoken to me about how doping had affected him and how it continued to haunt him, in spite of the fact he had come clean and was now racing without using banned drugs.

I shouldn't have lied. I shouldn't have called Floyd a liar when he had finally told the truth about the team and us. But I did.

Denying the allegation allowed me to go on and participate in the Tour de France for the first time, realising a lifelong goal. Yet even there, the dream was not reality. The stakes were higher, the pressures to perform were greater, the attention was unrelenting, but ultimately it was another bike race, on a grander scale. Instead of a few fans watching me race as an amateur, now there were millions of them. But the sensations and the emotions I felt as a rider were no different than in any of the other races I had ridden.

The moment of the three-week journey around France that meant the most to me was when we arrived in Paris, and I could see the Eiffel Tower in the distance. For a few seconds, or maybe even minutes, I floated in the middle of the bunch. The peloton had yet to ignite its charge towards the line, and I could pedal in the slipstream without applying pressure. I thought about my dad, and our trip to France when I was eight. Tears welled in my eyes. On that trip we had spent so many great, and pure, moments together on a bike. Through my life on a bike, I had complicated things immensely, and stacked up transgressions and regrets, by missing the essence of riding, the experience and what sport was truly about. I had failed to understand why it brought me so much happiness. Poor decisions in the pursuit of a career and results brought me grief, fear and guilt.

Arriving on the Champs-Elysées I scanned the massive crowd of thousands for my family as we lapped our way up and down the avenue to the Place de la Concorde. I knew they would be leaning on the barriers, near the start line, in the area reserved for those associated with teams and the organisation. On the third lap, I could hear screams of 'Papi!' above the clapping and cheering of the crowd and the noise of the race. I looked over my shoulder, and there they were, Liam and Ashlin, mouths wide open, smiles broad, faces red, yelling with gusto.

19

It is May 2012. Four months have passed since the Tour of Qatar and nine since I last raced in Europe. My body has recovered from the injuries. My broken leg and arm have healed well, and the enforced rest and time off my bike have rejuvenated me mentally and physically. At home, training consistently, without illness or distraction, I feel better than I have in a long time. The six weeks sitting idle in a wheelchair have been good for me in ways I would not have predicted. It has been my longest stretch without riding since I was a small boy. Even then, I was active, moving incessantly, as kids do.

The trip from the airport to the hotel is comforting in a way I have not before experienced. On the bus, looking out of the tinted window at the Norwegian countryside, I feel like a bike racer again. I sit comfortably in my seat – the seat I sat on so many times during the previous two years – and listen to my teammates chat about their last races, all of which I've missed. Through two Giros d'Italia and a Tour de France, the seat had been my spot. Now it feels as if I have regained my identity. But I am still not sure whether I want to be back racing. The time at home has been good. I have discovered a life that I never before knew, one in which the family is more content and secure. The children are more relaxed, with fewer upsets. The anxiety, the tension rooted in my peripatetic life has dissipated.

In the storage box beside the seat are bits and pieces left behind by other riders who have used the seat after the last race: pins, a set of numbers, an energy bar, one glove and a race book.

At home, training, I rediscovered something else I had lost progressively through my career. Once my injuries healed, I piled on hours of training. At first, I didn't follow a programme. The training was built on my internal sensations, having learned that, while trying to regain fitness after crashes, it was best not to follow someone else's guidelines but my own body's rhythms. Recovered, I stretched myself further the next day; worn, I rested. The formula was simple, but required that I push hard while also being honest with myself. Cyclists become good at deceiving themselves and others, believing their fitness or skills are better than they are. We do it because we are competitive, because we learn that we can't back down when weak, and that we must persist to do the job. Had I been dishonest with myself, the result would have been a fresh injury.

In the process, I rediscovered my desire to ride. It became wholly internal, as it had been when I was a young teen. A teammate told me that the team's management never expected me to race again after seeing the gravity of my injuries and knowing I planned to retire at the end of the season. The team would likely have understood if I'd decided to retire immediately. But instead, I trained to prove something to myself: that I wasn't broken, that I could return to racing and compete at the level to which I was accustomed. I also needed to retire on my own terms. I didn't want to finish my career in a hospital bed, but after crossing a finish line. My daily goals – to go from not being able to use my leg and arm to racing – fed my internal desire to ride to the best of my ability.

In the return to fitness, gains are exponential in the first two weeks. The challenge is as much mental as it is physical. I was climbing hills more slowly than I had in years. This would have been demoralising in other circumstances, but now I didn't really mind. I was just happy to be riding again. I unplugged my powermeter, stopped using a heart-rate monitor and simply rode. The powerful fluidity that I'd gained as a professional was gone. I was floundering like a weekend warrior, breathing hard on the hills without going fast. Each long climb was an accomplishment. A two-hour ride left me worn but elated. Over two weeks I accumulated kilometres, going from two to three to five hours. Until I felt ready, I didn't ride with professionals, but with Dede, with the fathers of my son's friends, and with my physiotherapist. And I rode alone. Like the boy I once was, when I tore through the Toronto neighbourhoods. I felt free, a liberty discovered anew after more than a month in a wheelchair and months of reflection. I digested every metre of countryside. On the bike, I felt like I was immersed in a novel and didn't want to miss a detail. It was something I hadn't felt in decades: appreciation for what I had, what I had been given, and the possibilities I enjoyed. I woke up eager to ride. I felt fatigue in my leg muscles, which until now I had missed. With the increasing kilometres of training, the aroma and flavour of food became more pronounced, and my appetite returned. I took none of it for granted but absorbed it as if every day was my last on a bike.

In my return to fitness, my body went through odd but predictable transitions. The first long hard ride left me in bits. I needed a warm bath to soothe my throbbing and twitching muscles. I devoured a feast in an attempt to satisfy my insatiable appetite. I awoke after a night's sleep feeling renewed, a feeling I will not experience again unless I stop riding for months. Today, I can ride for hours at a consistent tempo. I have regained my endurance, as if something that was dormant within me has woken. The next change occurs after two weeks of hard training, when I feel again as though I can physically handle the workload of a professional cyclist. This is the moment when the progress becomes less pronounced, when I climb more quickly by seconds, not minutes, when I must ride farther and harder to achieve minimal fitness gains. The greatest lift will come from the stimulus of racing. As my body becomes attuned to that workload, only the extreme demands of a hard tour or a training block in the high mountains for several days will extend my fitness further.

With a month of riding in my legs, I feel ready to train with professional cyclists, resuming a routine I left in Qatar. Before bed, messages are sent between Jez, David, a few others and me, deciding where and when to meet. The goal is a fairly long ride in the mountains with an hour of motorpacing at the end of the ride to stretch us out and simulate the speed of a race.

Outside the cafe, where we have met often in the last ten years, bikes are stacked against the wall like a pile of kids' bikes outside an ice-cream shop. On the patio, under the large stone arcades that enclose the *plaça*, a group of riders sit at a chromed metal table spotted with white coffee cups and plates of croissants. They sit like cyclists, slouching in chairs, some with their feet up on other chairs, using the armrests for support. Their physiques are lithe and tanned, their faces youthful but etched by the wind, scarred by crashes and lined by grimaces of joy, pain and sadness. Their characters lack the tension of the suit-wearing businessmen. Cyclists relax to prepare their bodies and minds for what is to come. Their colourful uniforms, each team's contrasting with the others against the grey stone walls, are apparent from across the dirt *plaça*. I am one of them, unique in the town, different from the cyclotourists who pass through on a short sojourn or the locals who dress up for their weekend rides. For months until now, I no longer felt as if I was. But the accumulated kilometres and the mental adaptation as I prepared myself to race again have brought me back into their world, closer to the bubble in which I will soon be reimmersed.

The route is decided, and we're off, up into the hills. Jez is resuming his training after a short break to recover from a nagging injury and the early season races. David is recovering from a broken collarbone. He fell with several other riders in the E3 Prijs, a race over cobbled roads in Belgium. The ambulance hauled them all off to the local hospital, which has become accustomed to dealing with torn and broken cyclists.

Ascending the climb, we find a rhythm that's comfortable for us all to sustain until the top, yet tough enough that we can no longer chat. The tempo hasn't been decided in discussion but is one we know from having ridden together so often. Hearing the more laboured breathing of a companion, we ease the pace. Together we try to get the most out of each other and ourselves. None of us has the fitness to climb quickly, but we are strong enough to sit and pedal without overworking or looking as if we're trying to muscle the bike in its battle with the gradient. We ease in and out of our saddles, in one movement, with a pedal stroke, a sway of the arms, a slight motion of the head, elbows and hands. We shift our bodies with the bikes, change gears without thought, all to maintain the tempo we have set. In near unison our turning legs tick over like the swing of a metronome. It is a rhythm we try to maintain over the undulations in the road.

At the summit, we pull on our jackets to conserve our warmth against the cool air. Then, like kids, we tear down the mountain. Together we go faster than I would have gone alone. We use each other's draught, follow each other's line, and reach the speed of a race. With each passing kilometre the temperature warms. In fifteen kilometres we're again in the valley, sweating, riding through the apple orchards and sprinting for a town sign.

Back in Girona, the scooter driver meets us at a service station. As he pulls up we sit on a kerb, filling our bottles, sipping Cokes and eating chocolate bars. We chat as we scroll through our mobile phones, looking at the messages that have arrived while we rode. The sun is now low in the sky. With four hours in our legs, the bars become a treat as well as a source of fuel. We set off, now finding a new tempo behind the scooter, the three of us rotating in its draught. Over the hilltops we sprint against each other, the scooter our carrot that we pursue as it lures us close to the point of exhaustion.

In the slipstream of the scooter, I am reminded of the sessions north of Toronto behind my father's 1954 Lambretta. Dressed in a bumblebee-yellow mechanic's jumpsuit, he took me out in the evenings after he closed the shop for a thrashing ride through the farmland that still surrounded the ever-encroaching city. As he accelerated, the scooter spluttered and then revved and roared. Cautious, I would leave a small gap between it and my front wheel as I anticipated my father's shifting of the gears and the ensuing lurch of the scooter. But I often touched its rear fender with my front tyre, buzzing the metal and burning off a line of paint. The strong stench of two-stroke exhaust permeated my clothing. By the night's end, my shins and shoes were dotted with splatters of motor oil, my legs ached with the same inner burn of a race, and, although only alone in the country with my dad, I felt like we had stolen moments of liberty that few other people in the city would ever experience. Drivers tooted a friendly beep, walkers gazed and cyclists watched in awe or cheered as we whirled by. Each time I rode behind the scooter, I felt the same elation at the session's end. Now, with Jez and David, it's no different.

Reaching an intersection where a left turn leads us home and a right takes us north around another eighty-kilometre loop, David and I look at each other and go right. Alone, we would have each gone home; together we agree to go farther. Feeling peer pressure, Jez follows.

On the last ascent up the small mountain to our home, I can feel the distance in my legs, arms and lungs. I've worked harder in one day than I have in months. For me, it is another step toward my goal, and it gives me the confidence to push myself even harder and to tell the team I am ready to race in the Tour of Norway.

The team bus arrives at the hotel. I feel oddly out of place, as if I am coming to a party without an invitation. Everyone, including the commissaires and race officials, chats as if they have only just seen each other a few nights ago, which they likely have, at another race, in another place. I am again a foreigner in their world, slowly reintegrating, still somewhat insecure with my fitness. It doesn't matter how well I have trained, I always wonder how well I will race. At home, I can control the variables. In a race, I have no idea how fit the peloton will be, how bad the weather or how hard we will compete. Those concerns provide the challenge. The stories on the bus, at the dinner table and in the hotel room about recent races and performances have made me feel even more insecure. I have barely pushed the extremes in training that my teammates have been reaching almost daily. But at least I have the motivation again of a novice while they are already feeling the wear of the season.

Walking down the hotel hall, I see the race from a different perspective. How odd it is that dirty laundry sits in bags in the hallway; that a large plastic bin of cereals, energy bars and fruit and a cooler full of drinks sit beside a door; that doors are left open while riders lie naked on massage tables with only a hand towel between their legs, being rubbed down with oil; that lists with the room number of every rider and staff member are posted in the elevators, and that riders lie in their beds with the television on, music blasting from speakers as they type away on their laptops and tap at mobile phones. The race has taken over the hotel. It feels totally removed from the outside world.

At the start of the race, the nervous fears flutter through my stomach. To feel in control of something, I play with my bike's position, adjusting it and then readjusting it, yet never completely comfortable. With a number on my back, I feel different on my bike, as if I am sitting differently, as if my legs are a little more potent, as if I can suddenly push the pedals harder and suffer more than I have in training. Pedalling around the start/ finish area, I wonder if that power will ever materialise. I fear I will be overly cautious in the speeding peloton.

Soon after the start, I ride to the side in the peloton, near the kerb, looking for an escape route if something happens, envisioning the crash in Qatar. In every roundabout, traffic island or pothole, I can see danger, and I back off. But to overcome our fears, we must face them. With the first attack and the increase in speed, I look for protection in the slipstream as the peloton draws out into a long thin line. On the wheel, I am not ready yet to place blind faith in the riders in front of me. That will come with the passing kilometres. The job requires it of me.

With a leader who can win, I am asked by the directeur to ride on the front. Soon afterward, a teammate joins me to share the workload. At the front, I settle into a rhythm. It is then I feel the energy of the race, and the effort, my ego being nourished by the knowledge that we are catching the riders in front, and that those behind are suffering and struggling to find shelter from the wind as the pace increases. The sensation of speed as we race down a hillside and along the plains is sublime; I feed it with a constantly escalating pressure. I sink lower on my bike as the race amplifies the sensation of speed. The countdown of kilometres and approaching finish line apply an unrelenting force while the crushing energy of the peloton devours the distance. At the front of that charge, where cameras focus, I am alight. With two kilometres to go, in a nearly five-hour race, I pull off the front of the peloton, unable to give any more of myself but knowing I have given enough. Job done. Satisfied.

At the end of the stage, I climb aboard the bus and immediately plunk down in the seat. Riders line up for the shower, each with a dark blue towel wrapped around his waist, torsos pale white, arms, necks and faces deep dark brown. Sunscreen has little effect under the sun after five or six sweaty hours. Some riders sip on recovery drinks. Others gulp soft drinks, although we're told to avoid them because they fill us up with chemicals and sugars that we don't need. But at the end of a long day they fulfil a craving for liquids. In the back of the bus, the doctor cares for a rider who has been injured in a crash. He scrubs the wounds clean in the shower and patches him up. Tomorrow is another day and another race.

The line to the shower shortens. I strip down, grab a towel from the neat pile in the locker at the back of the bus and wash off. Some riders sit in their chairs with only a towel around their waist, eating bowls of rice. Others, dressed in their team gear, are punching away at their mobile phones. The television at the front of the bus is still showing the race. We have already watched the replay of the finish over and over again. Our own commentary is often far more accurate and animated than the announcer's. On the way to the hotel, we watch the stage yet again, reliving what we have just experienced but from a different angle that makes it all look oddly flat. Television can never capture the speed, the gradient, or the aggression in the peloton as it races to the finish.

Someone turns the music up in the bus. I can feel the thump of the bass in my seat and through my feet. The song takes us away to another place. Like a bunch of teenagers hanging out after school, we sing along, tapping our feet and bopping our heads, joyously being transported somewhere outside the race for a few short minutes. High from the post-race endorphin rush, we laugh and joke in a way that never happens at any other time. The stage over, we have a few hours to relax before we begin mentally preparing ourselves for the next stage. We will soon be at the hotel. The first thing we will ask about is the condition of the rooms. We will only be there for one night, but a nice bed makes a big difference after a hard day of racing, even if we lie in it for only a few hours.

In the hotel, I look at the tourists and feel mildly jealous of their lives. They're under no obligation to get up and race tomorrow for hours. They can relax, go to the hotel pool, sit by the sea or go for a hike in the mountains. We can never relax. The race gnaws at us constantly. We cannot escape from it, even when we watch a movie or read a book. My mind is immersed in the race. Everything else is just a momentary distraction.

Walking through the lobby, I sense the stares of the tourists and business people. I can't help but notice the sharp contrast in the lobby between the cyclists and the suits. I feel that I have regained my identity and my place on the team. But I question whether I want to maintain this identity. My perspective and priorities have shifted.

20

Through my last racing season, I had planned for my retirement but the transition away from professional cycling isn't as simple as I had imagined. I spoke often about the change with Steve Peters, our team psychiatrist. He advised me, guided me and comforted me. The injuries I had suffered early in the year only reinforced my decision to stop. The time away from the races, with my family, made me realise how much happier we all were together. For me, as a father and husband, the sacrifice was too great; I didn't want to be away from them, I no longer wanted to risk continued damage to my body, and although I enjoyed the thrill of the race, my fear slowed me in situations where before I had accelerated. Through the season, I had time to reflect and to decide what to do next. I believed I would again find something that evoked the same thrilling emotions as a race, the positive feelings that had helped me push through pain, frustration, defeat and fear of injury. Knowing it would soon be over and my final race day was imminent, I embraced those last moments on the bus with my teammates; I kept my race jerseys with the numbers pinned on, realising they might some day be cherished relics; I immersed myself in the present, absorbing my surroundings. The pressure of another season and another contract wasn't there. It gave me a new perspective on the life inside and outside of the circus in which I had been a performer.

Throughout the year, riding with mates, with Dede and alone, I realised the joy I derived on the bike was something that I could hold on to whether or not there was a number on my back. The elements that made up a race – tearing down a mountain pass, pounding my way up a climb, thumping over cobbles or reaching a finish line – could be a part of any ride. Without a helicopter above me, a headphone in my ear and a television camera in front capturing the moment, the experience is more profound as it is untainted. Out with friends, the finish lines are still there, as are the climbs, yet the experience is more personal and internally driven. This is the spiritual side of cycling that is lost in the business of pro racing. And this is what I love more than anything. Cycling will always be part of my life, as long as I can pedal.

Since I first began racing I thought I would be forced to retire as my body gave out to the workload and my performance declined. But with each season, as I learned to train more effectively and to race with greater intelligence, I recovered more quickly, my endurance improved and I was as fit as I had ever been. Mentally, however, the demands had worn me down. I felt relieved to be nearing the end.

My goal was to perform in my final races in Canada, where I had started. Through my career as a professional, I rarely had the opportunity to race at home. Bookending my career at home was how I wanted to finish. I went to the Nationals in Lac-Mégantic, Quebec, with my father in late June, as I had when I was younger. It gave the two of us an opportunity to share an adult moment at a race. I didn't have teammates, mechanics or soigneurs to work with or care for me. My dad did some of that as he had when I was a boy.

The course was the same as I had ridden in my first National Championships road race twenty-two years before. Little had changed in the area. Roads had been paved, the town had modernised, but the aromas, the woods and the thrashing summer storms took me back to my adolescence. I rode with the exuberance of a kid, and although I was the strongest on the day, I was outnumbered in the tactical game, as is so often the case in a bike race, and I finished second.

Through a torrential storm we drove north towards Quebec City airport, on a straight road through the tree-covered rolling hills of eastern Quebec. I recognised the terrain from previous races, a decade or more before. The towns reminded me of teammates and finish lines, and I wondered if I would ever see them again.

Even decades later, places I have been evoke specific emotions, the way a scent arouses an image or the sight of chain grease on hands returns me to my father's shop. Those moments and emotions have taught me lessons and matured me. I may have suppressed them, but by releasing them and speaking about them, I feel liberated.

During our drive west, we stopped in Saint-Georges, a small town I knew well. There was a festival on, and the streets were full of people. Bands played, kids bounced in inflatable castles, and everybody seemed to know one another. We sat outdoors on a patio as the summer sun turned to a bright orange before it set. I devoured a burger and fries and guzzled a beer, and then another, satiating the hunger of the race and enjoying the few hours when I could relax and didn't yet have to think about the next objective. On the patio, my father and I chatted about racing. When I was a boy my mom had grown frustrated by our incessant dinnertime conversations about bikes and racing. But as I immersed myself in the sport, and as I began to understand the reality of life in the pro peloton, and then when I used performance-enhancing drugs, those conversations began to fade away. I no longer wanted to speak about the races as I once did, because they'd consumed every aspect of my life. I wanted to escape from that life, not delve further into it. I didn't want to lie to my parents and ruin their image of me. I was embarrassed by what I had become a part of and by what I had done. I wanted them to remain proud of me, and of the sport that had inspired my father since he was young. Now I realised I'd been misguided in hiding.

As we sat at the table over our bacon burgers and beer, I wanted to tell my dad about all my experiences, good and bad, to share it all with him as I once had, before things changed. But I didn't. As I had so many other times, I wanted to open up, to ask for forgiveness, to be honest, but I feared the consequences. Instead I bottled it up and moved the conversation on. Soon I would be back in Europe, racing in my final races on the continent. I would learn later that my cowardice had more severe consequences than my honesty ever would have done.

With each passing race I felt as if I was slowly departing to another life. I received job offers. The most interesting was from Team Sky, who offered me a position in marketing and communications. I was excited about the proposal. It would not only allow me to stay in cycling but also give me the opportunity to learn and expand my skills. I was in good shape. I wanted to finish my cycling career well before I moved on to another stimulating phase of my life. I wanted to remember my final races with fondness and compete in them with guts and heart.

But in early July I crashed again, breaking my arm in the same place I had broken it in Qatar in February. I had asked the surgeon then what would happen if I fell on it again. Referring to the X-ray, he pointed to the screw holding the plate in my arm and said, 'It will break here.' The crash in July occurred at the end of a hard day of racing in heat and humidity. A rider bumped another in the sprint finish and brought the rest of us down like dominoes. From the left kerb to the right, we tumbled. I braked hard but I hit a falling rider and sailed over the handlebars. I put my arm down on the pavement to protect my face and head, and in that split second I knew it would break. When I landed, I felt it snap at the weakest point, where the doctor had said it would. The metal he had so carefully screwed in place stuck out of my elbow at an odd angle. I got up, as riders whizzed by and crossed the finish line. My broken arm limp, pushing my twisted and fractured bike with my other arm, I walked across the finish line, officially finishing the race, on my way to the ambulance.

This time I resigned myself to fate. I didn't feel demoralised or frustrated, but pragmatic. There was still time to rebuild, to finish off the season in Canada. I wouldn't be flying, but I could be fit enough to compete, do my job and race with panache one last time.

In Girona, the recovery routine began once again. Unable to ride, I ran up a mountain behind our house as hard as my legs and lungs would carry me, up the rocky path, under the searing Catalan sun, as the cicadas hissed and buzzed. The effort felt good. Four days a week, I spent two hours in physiotherapy. Then I began riding. Soon I was fit enough to race again. The team directeurs scheduled my return for the Grands Prix of Quebec and Montreal. My arm ached, and it swelled slightly after a ride, but I could tolerate the pain, especially to race one last time in Canada. I returned to Toronto ten days before the races to adjust to the time zone and to spend time with my family.

That was when USADA called to ask me to testify. I'd known the call would come. I had anticipated it since I'd first used performance-enhancing drugs. But I could never have prepared myself for it. Like the crashes, the call would leave an ugly scar.

I set off for the race. In Toronto airport, with my wife, our children and my parents, I felt uneasy. My stomach was heavy. I didn't know what to expect. My parents had no clue what was going on, other than the little I had told them: that USADA had called me to ask about the period that I rode with US Postal. My parents had asked why and what I knew. I avoided their questions, shrugging my shoulders and changing the subject.

I called a family friend who is a lawyer in Toronto, as the USADA attorney, Bill Bock, had recommended. I told him few details, but said that I needed representation. He advised me to speak with a US attorney who was familiar with the case. I also spoke to George Hincapie. I knew he had already testified, and I told him that I had been contacted. I asked if he could recommend a lawyer. After a multitude of calls, emails and conversations, in airports and then in a quiet corner of the race hotel away from my teammates and peers, I worked to find someone who could advise me on the formalities of the process.

The imminent races were constantly present in my thoughts. The team, my family and cycling fans expected little of me. I was only just returning from a broken arm and extensive surgery. My team would not have been surprised if I had climbed off an hour or more before the race finished. They would have been more surprised if I'd finished at all. For them, I would have achieved enough just by having the fitness to start and work for the team in the first half of the race. But for me that wouldn't be enough. In my last races in Canada, I had far greater expectations.

I wanted to feel the thrill one last time, to see the smiles on the roadside, to hear the Canadians cheer and to be up front, at least for a few moments, for our sons. They had rarely seen me race, and this was likely their final opportunity. I had no idea what to expect, but I would end the day knowing I had given it my very best.

On the start line in Quebec, my unease remained. I found it hard to stand in front of an audience knowing that I would soon tell them I had lied and cheated. But there was a job to be done, teammates to help and a race to ride. For most involved, this day was no different from any other race in any long season in our careers, but for me it had become very personal.

Soon after we set off, I was back in the bubble, moving as I had since I was a boy, in the belly of the peloton, feeling and seeing its ebb and flow, watching my rivals move, and breaking down the pieces of the race that would make it whole. The race was my focus, although with each lap of the ten-kilometre circuit I looked for our sons and Dede in the crowd to give them a quick smile.

As the race wore on, the peloton shrank. The repeated ascents through the old town in Quebec and the accelerations out of the tight corners drained riders' legs until they were mercilessly dropped. I could feel the titanium plate screwed to my arm as I climbed out of the saddle, gripped my handlebars tightly and pumped hard on the pedals. On the flatter sections of the course, I massaged the bone in an attempt to relieve the ache. With each passing lap, a point on the scar swelled into a disconcerting lump. I wondered if one of the ten screws was coming out and the plate was moving, like a loose hinge on a door. But I pushed aside the thought that I might damage my arm. I was going to finish and finish well.

In the final lap, the group was small, and I was in it. Among the leading finishers, mine was just another name. But I had seen the smiles on my boys' faces, and their embrace after the finish was golden.

From Quebec, we moved west to Montreal by train for the second of the two races. I spoke with journalists about my imminent retirement, what my career had meant to me, and what was next. Considering what was coming, my answers felt loaded. A month later, the same journalists would call to interview me for another story.

The course in Montreal was one I knew well. I had competed there several times, and two decades before I had watched starstruck as my childhood idols raced on it. It was there that I had first seen Lance Armstrong race, as a neophyte. I had heard his veteran teammate Phil Anderson reprimand him with terse obscenity for making a juvenile tactical mistake. I chuckled as the Australian scolded the brash American and wondered if Lance would ever amount to much as a pro. A year later, Lance had become the team's leader. I watched the Italian icon Gianni Bugno ride up Mont Royal in his big chain ring. His bike lurched slowly beneath him but he moved unfathomably fast. Each of his pedal strokes exuded inspiring potency. These were the moments that the photos and videos I had watched so closely often failed to capture.

Early in the race, I climbed the same hill, in the dead centre of the peloton. I gazed at the spectators at the roadside, saw myself in a young teenager, and wondered if his thoughts and impressions were the same as mine had once been.

For the last few laps I held on, suffering more from the pain in my arm than the effort on the climb. I moved in the bunch and around the corners with apprehension, always a few bike lengths from the wheel in front of me to avoid danger. My arm began aching enough to make every movement worrisome.

The ache made me wonder if I would ride my final metres as a professional bike racer in Montreal. I was scheduled to race through the end of the season, but I didn't want to undergo any more surgeries or physiotherapy. I had had enough. I didn't want to push through pain any longer.

On the final lap, my teammate Lars Petter Nordhaug jumped away from the peloton and won the sprint for first. At the finish we were elated. It was his first major victory and it proved the talent we had all seen during our training camps and through the season. Through proper coaching, the team had nurtured his physical talents, and he was now producing results, bringing much-needed publicity in the process.

We embraced each other as the cameras flashed and microphones pressed into our midst. In a small way, I had contributed to the victory by doing my work as a teammate. I finished in the middle of the front pack, fifty-seventh. Moments after the finish, I sat in the press room alongside my teammates and rivals. Outside the tent, the sun set and clouds rolled in.

Pedalling back to the hotel through the Montreal traffic, I chatted with cycling commuters at stop lights and signed a few autographs. The race over, my legs felt lighter. I coasted down the hill that led to the hotel, absorbing the post-race moment that I had cherished for years in a way I had never done before. A block or two from the hotel, I rode past the headquarters of the World Anti-Doping Authority and my thoughts drifted from the race to the case.

I called Fran Millar, who was part of the Team Sky management, to tell her I would testify. She understood. She had lived through something similar with her brother, David. I promised her I would let the team know how the case progressed. She said she would alert the team principals and corporation.

Before I testified, I finally told my parents, family and a few close friends that I had used performance-enhancing drugs for a period in my career. I explained to our children the lessons I had learned from my mistakes. With each admission, I felt drained, but better. On 4 October, I testified over several hours in a telephone conference with USADA and my lawyers. When I hung up, I closed my eyes, said a prayer and took several deep breaths. A liberating sense of relief washed over me. I had taken another turn.

Days later, just before my testimony was made public, I received an email from a journalist. He knew I had testified, but he didn't know what I'd said. 'Hang in there today,' he wrote. 'I'd say spend the whole day out on a good bike ride if you can.'

Tears welled up in my eyes and rolled down my face, uncontrolled – a lost child's tears. There was nothing I wanted more than to be out on my bike, eluding what I was soon to face, the barrage of interview requests, emails, phone calls and questions. Ironically it was the bike that had taken me to this point in my life, and it was the bike that I wished for now more than anything else: to ride away and escape. But I stayed at home, on the couch, in front of my computer, waiting to respond to requests for interviews from all over the world and feeling buoyed by unexpected and thoughtful emails from people from whom I hadn't heard in years.

From the window, I could see parents picking up their children from the school across the street. Many of the parents were also our friends. Today, Dede would pick up our boys, take them to the park to play and then take them out to dinner so I could focus on the interviews.

The following morning I stepped away from my computer and went out of the house. I rode my bike. I jumped on the trampoline. I ate lunch in the garden with Dede. In the late afternoon, I walked apprehensively across the road to pick up the boys from school, no longer feeling like Michael the bike racer, but Michael the guy who doped. Two of the fathers walked towards me. I expected vilification but what they gave me was a tender hug.

21

A warm spring breeze blew through the open kitchen window. The boys played outdoors, jumping on the trampoline in shorts and T-shirts. A bead of sweat dripped down my neck. Ten minutes of bouncing with them had left me sweating and slightly winded. My fitness was far from what it was half a year ago. Chugging a glass of water, I sat at the kitchen counter as Dede prepared dinner. Liam ran inside and asked to get the hose and sprinkler out. I resisted. It still didn't seem warm enough and I didn't want him to catch a chill.

The Toronto winter had been long. People talked about the weather constantly. The hope for clear days, for sunshine, is universal. After years in Spain the Canadian climate had made our transition to Toronto tough. In the ice, snow and cold, I rode my bike less than ever, which wasn't good for my head. I needed to ride more.

Another glass of water went down. I rolled up my jeans to cool off a bit. My legs looked like somebody else's. They had lost their definition, the once visible veins hidden under a layer of fat. Most oddly, for the first time in my life, my legs were covered in a thick coat of hair. Ever since I was a teenager I had shaved them clean. High-school classmates made jokes at first but then respectfully understood that shaved legs symbolised who I was and what I did. Through the winter, with no reason to ride, with boxes to unpack, children to settle in new schools and a life to sort out, I had neglected them. But seeing them now, I could no longer accept their condition, not because they were unsightly but because I had let go of something I never thought I would: my identity as a cyclist. I missed being one. Having not ridden my bike in months, I realised how much I loved it.

Even though I wasn't riding, I had watched the Classics and early-season races on television. I cheered for my old teammates. The races didn't make me long for the peloton as I thought they might. I watched with interest but not with desire. If I missed anything about the racing, it was simply being with a group of guys, being a part of something unique, something that inspired people. But I had never once regretted retiring.

When I finally put my leg back over my bike to ride with the local club, I realised what I'd missed most. I had forgotten the feeling of being on the wheel: the surge and the relief. Arriving home I felt lighter, cleaner, more focused, more energetic and happier.

I don't need racing. I just need to ride.

Spending time with my father at his shop, I rediscovered more of what I had missed. On a ride home from his shop, through a moonlit park, we chatted as we had when I was a boy, a teenager and then a young adult. He is older and greyer, but still rides with the same spirit. He seems most content when he is on his bike. Decades ago, we'd ridden home together along the same path, after we'd worked together to build a bike. I was in fifth grade, and we were building the bike I would ride to and from school daily. It was green, my favourite colour. It had generator lights, a fixed wheel and mudguards. Once or twice a week after school, I went to the shop to build the bike with him. My father taught me how to cut the tubes, then braze and file the joints. The bike now hangs from a hook on the ceiling in his shop with a collection of the other bikes I've used in my lifetime.

That collection shows the dramatic evolution of bicycles through my career. The first bike I rode, the one that Ashlin now rides, is steel, has a five-speed cogset on the back and is similar to those ridden by professionals in the 1980s. In fact, it's not much different from bikes ridden in the 1950s. The bike works as well as it did thirty years ago, even after a dozen kids raced on it until it became too small for them. Until I was twenty, my father made almost all of the frames I rode. Like a tailor, he measured my body, cut the tubes to length and set the angles to make the bike fit properly. Until the 1990s all top cyclists rode custom-made frames. But craftsmanship was replaced when bikes made of aluminium, carbon, scandium and titanium mass-produced in large Asian factories became the norm.

I started with toe clips and straps, cagelike contraptions that locked my shoes in place, with shoe plates nailed to the soles. Then I moved on to clipless pedals, which worked like ski bindings. For a decade, my bikes had gear levers on the downtubes, which were succeeded by gear levers integrated into the brake levers. Now riders could shift gears without taking their hands off the handlebars. More recently, electric connections allow seamless shifting at the touch of a button.

In the 1980s and '90s, bicycles became more aerodynamic. Cables were tucked into the handlebars and tubes to streamline the bike. Time-trial wheels became solid discs. Spokes were bladed, and time-trial handlebars positioned the rider like a skier, arms tight and close together, so that he or she could slice through the air. Clothing was made tighter, out of new fabrics.

In Annemasse, I rode an aluminium frame and then moved on to a carbon bike, which was stiffer, lighter and faster. As a professional, I rode on the best equipment. I felt as if I was riding a new bike every day. Everything felt clean and crisp. The mechanics replaced parts before they began to show wear and adjusted them daily to make sure they worked properly and that nothing failed. We kept bikes at home, race bikes, spare bikes and time-trial bikes. Team trucks were loaded with equipment, and we had warehouses filled with more bikes, equipment, vehicles and supplies.

For different conditions and terrain we used different wheels. On the flat, there were aerodynamic carbon wheels. For the mountains, where every gram counts, there were lightweight carbon wheels with special tyres. For the cobbled classics, there were more resilient wheels with larger tyres to better resist punctures and absorb some of the vibration.

Initially, I felt elated with the new bikes and new technologies. But the thrill was short-lived. Before long they simply became tools.

Riding home from the shop, my dad uses the commuter bike he put together twenty years earlier. A few times a week, when he ventures out with his mates, he rides a road bike that he built for himself almost thirty years ago. A few parts have been upgraded, but it remains essentially the same bike. People assume that a bike-shop owner and frame builder would have the newest and the fanciest of bikes. But function is my father's priority. If it works, why change it? Novelty doesn't necessarily mean improvement.

As we rode along the path we passed two teenagers on discount-store mountain bikes. One rode without hands, the other pedalled away with his shirt off. They were clearly happy, laughing and chatting. Moments later, a cyclist on a fancy carbon bike with all the latest equipment passed us, equally content. As long as the bike works and fits well, the emotion is the same. Speed is relative. Victory is fleeting. But the ride can last forever.

My father has lived his life this way. Oddly, at the other end of my career, I realise it more than ever now, as we ride together.

The constant pursuit was what made me persist through a career of ups and downs. Reflecting in retirement I wonder why I didn't stop sooner, when I broke my back for the first time, when I began to understand the pervasiveness of drug use, when I crashed again and again. I had never considered the accumulation of it all. I'd spent my career on a bike, deep in the guts of sport, until I testified to USADA. I told the lawyers my story from start to finish. At the end of it, my lawyer said, 'That's one hell of a narrative.' My dream had been simple, a path to stardom, yet the reality was far more complex, richer and nuanced.

I rode on because I had promised myself that I would quit the moment my progression stopped. But progression never stops. I learned with each experience, good or bad, and I matured to the point where even in my last years the progression continued. I was constantly reinvigorated to start again, to accept the challenge and persist.

I rode on because, after persisting through the toughest moments, when frustrations could paralyse my will, my will grew stronger and the ecstasy of the achievement more profound. With each challenge, the ambitions I had harboured since I'd first started riding a bike took on new meaning. They evolved over time. They began as superficial reactions to accolades, headlines and trophies, but they progressed into maturing experiences. If success had come too easily, I might have quit racing sooner, but the lifelong commitment, the small victories, the joy of reaching the finish line, the half hour in the bus with my legs up after the race, listening to music and my teammates' chatter, riding for hours without realising the passing of time, made everything we ploughed through secondary.

Speaking with my retired teammates, George and Jez, I find that they have also tried to find the same equilibrium in their lives. They continue to ride, no longer focused on a finish line. Not only do they ride to maintain some level of fitness, but also because it gives them an unparalleled sense of fulfilment.

Climbing back on my bike after months seems to put things straight. Pedalling is therapy.

22

The front door opens. From the dining room, I can hear the clunk of snowboots and the zip zip zip of the nylon ski jacket.

Hi Papi! Can we go for a ride?

Hi Tugsy! Sure.

I give him a hug, enveloping his torso in my arms and kissing him on the cheek. His smooth face is flushed red from the cool spring air. The winter has been tough, longer than usual. The grey, dirty snow banks have lined the streets into the spring. Patches of icy snow spot shady places under trees. As he enters the room a waft of fresh air follows him in. Holding him in my arms, I realise it is his odour, from the day spent outside on the playground, sweating, playing in the dirt and rolling in the frozen dirty grass. There is sweetness to the smell, one he will soon lose, like his older brother and the rest of us. It is the smell that every manufactured perfume fails to capture.

How was your day? I ask. His boots have a thick layer of mud and snow in the tread.

I haven't been outside all day. Just months ago I would have spent hours on my bike under the grey sky and cold spitting rain. Now retired, I have no desire to move out of the warmth of the house. I no longer have to. As a professional, on the days I didn't ride due to the weather or illness or injury, I felt guilty. The guilt would haunt me through the day, relieved only by a physical effort. It didn't matter how much I pushed myself as long as I moved a bit.

Dede comes into the house. A fresh rush of cold air. She

puts down Ashlin's backpack, pulls out his empty lunch box, his homework and his winter mitts. I have grown to love the daily routine. We never had one while I was racing. In a few minutes, the school bell will ring across the street and it will be time to pick up Liam. At the pick-up, the parents will chat outside while the kids kick balls, climb walls, swing from the jungle gym and race each other up and down the field. While racing, I would drop in and out, be gone for weeks and home for days, never quite settling in anywhere. My routine was one of constant change that the family fought to fit into their lives.

Ashlin is eager to ride. He's asked me four times in less than a minute. Dede tells me she will pick up Liam. Ashlin runs, jumps, up the stairs to his bedroom. He's soon back down, now out of his school uniform and wearing sweatpants and a Sky jersey with his name printed down the side, as mine once was. Underneath, he's wearing a fleece, the tight jersey containing its puffiness on his torso while his arms bulge like some oddly disproportioned cartoon superhero.

Where are my Sky gloves?

In your helmet by the back door, Dede answers.

I tell him to put on a thin pair of wool gloves underneath the racing gloves to keep his hands warm. He disagrees and argues that his hands will be warm enough. I tell him again that without them his hands will freeze. He won't have it. He wants to wear the Sky gloves. I shift tactics and try to change his mind by saying that when I was racing we would wear thin gloves under our racing gloves. Not convinced, he pulls on his short-fingered Lycra racing gloves.

We have a loop we do after school, when the weather is good enough and when nothing else is going on. Ashlin rides the bike my father made for me as a gift for my sixth birthday. The frame and the parts are all scaled to size. It's painted green and yellow to match the frames of my father's bike shop's racing team. The day after I got it, we went for a ride in the park, which was then blanketed in deep snow. I rode in my snow boots, toque and parka but felt like a professional racing in Belgium.

As soon as we are down the street, Ashlin is already speeding ahead, holding the drops of his bars, out of the saddle to accelerate from the stop signs and back as he maintains the speed on the flats. As he pedals I can see the effort in his face, and then he stops, coasts for a second or two, smiles, rests and pushes out another spurt. He's yelling and encouraging me.

Papi, don't slow down. Go as fast as you did when you were in the Olympics that time and finished eighth.

He jumps his bike over the speed bumps, his wheel gaining a few centimetres of air. It probably feels like much more to him. People in the street pause to watch him pass. Perhaps because the scaled-down bike makes him look like a sized-down pro, or perhaps because of his smile and his effervescence as he thrashes away at the pedals. There are few cars. I alert him to the parked ones for fear he will look down and pile into one, as I did when I was his age, sprinting with my head down, trying to emulate the professionals sprinting the final metres of a race.

The bite of the cold air begins to sting my face. Ashlin's cheeks are now a brighter shade of red than they were when he came home. At the far end of our loop, a few kilometres from the house, he begins to slow. He doesn't complain but I can see he is no longer holding the handlebars with the same tight grip. He's also lost his confidence in the corners, as his hands are now too cold to use the brakes properly. I tell him to stop by the kerb.

My hands are cold, Paps. Let's shorten the loop, but not go straight back, just a little bit shorter.

I tell him that in only a few minutes we will be home. I try to warm his hands with a little friction and put them in my gloves. He pulls them off, gets back on his bike and pushes off from the kerb. He's sprinting ahead again, and I chase to catch up. I can see myself as a boy in him. There is beauty in the sense of freedom and joy he exudes. Pure internally driven enthusiasm to go faster, to go farther, to test his limits, to break through them and to discover something beyond. It is where all professional cyclists start, before we face the external pressures placed on us by society, family, coaches, friends. It keeps us pushing through hard moments, when we are suffering, when we are struggling, when the pressures wear us down. The emotions, the internal drive, kept me riding and kept me wanting more of it.

I don't care if he ever rides a bike professionally. On many levels, I would prefer that he didn't, particularly if he has to face what our generation and others have had to deal with. Professional cycling is evolving, but change has been slow. I am still far too aware of the realities that athletes confront as they race towards their goals. Dede and I have often discussed our boys' futures and whether we should encourage their athletic pursuits. We wonder if, one day, they will have what it takes to become professionals. Their dreams are precious. We will support them, encourage them and protect them, but their drive will remain their own.

As a parent, I hope they will never face the same decisions, the same injuries or the same heartbreak of realising that reality does not resemble the dream. The culture of cycling and all sports needs to change, and I trust it will, as the misdeeds of past generations become more apparent. As our stories are told, I trust that we will all take more responsibility for our children's futures and for athletes' health. Society's expectations have been misguided.

We have lost sight of the true meaning of sport. We expect records to be broken, and we feel disappointed when they aren't. Crowds cheer for fighting hockey players. We embrace, encourage and promote risk. We expect our national athletes to win dozens of Olympic medals. When they don't, we regard them as failures, even though they have represented our country honourably and done their best. We live in a society where health is secondary to performance and our best is not good enough unless we win. I don't want my children to be part of it.

As we wind our way through the neighbourhoods, he hammers away at the pedals, but says little. We pass his friend's house, where he usually looks for their cat curled up on the porch, but today he passes without a word or hesitation in his pedal stroke. Only a few blocks from home, he looks over at me and says, 'I really had my heart set on those nachos.' And he smiles. It is a line from a movie he has just seen, his mind skipping to it to escape the discomfort of his cold hands. These are the mind games that we play with ourselves, one that I played so many times during my career on a bike, to block out discomfort, refocusing, to turn a negative thought into a positive.

I laugh with him, at his quirky humour. Another ten or twenty hard pedal strokes and we are on the home stretch. He gets out of the saddle and begins the final sprint. The finish line is a road sign, metres from our home. Rolling up the driveway, he plunks down the bike on a dirty snow pile that has been around for a month or so.

He warms up inside the house, telling his mom all about the ride, how he got cold, how he went faster around the loop, how he made it up the hill without help and how he wants to do it again tomorrow.

23

The steep and winding descent flattens and edges along a small lake. Cottages spot the shore: specks of brown on green, sitting on an Oxford blue lake and covered by a true blue sky. Motorboats tied to docks bob ever so slightly on the calm water. There is no wind. Gravel kicks up from the wheels in front of me, as they crunch on the rock and dirt surface and then spit up pebbles. The dense Muskoka woods form an umbrella of green above the road, shielding it and us from the summer sun. The descent carries us halfway up the next climb, when we have to start pedalling again to push over the top and back down to the shore.

On the climb we are side by side. Dede is sitting lower on the saddle to keep the rear wheel from spinning on the loose gravel. Her face shows a slight grimace: eyes scrunched, mouth tight and then open wide to inhale full lungs of air. Sweat beads have formed on her nose, something I have always thought is oddly cute. It is the same expression I saw when we first met, fifteen years ago, and were riding up Lefthand Canyon in Colorado. Before that, I had seen the gritting face in cycling magazines.

In the last eight years, since our first son was born, our rides together have been infrequent, as I was away racing, and she was home taking care of the boys, embracing the Catalan culture, studying Spanish and later completing her MBA. We were both busy, and our lives contrasted in many ways. When we did ride, we never went out for longer than two hours. We rode at an easy conversational speed. On the bike we could catch up on everything that was lost in our life's daily routines. Often, the conversations we had while riding were better than any we had on any sort of date night.

At the top of the hill, we pull over to check a map. We've both become nagged by the feeling of being off track and lost. The only signs we have seen point to snowmobile trails. Any others simply say, 'No trespassing.'

We are well off our planned route. But that doesn't matter. Turning around, we ride a short distance to another dirt road that, we hope, will lead us in the right direction. Lakes are our points of reference as the woods are too dense to see any other significant landmarks.

Through the spring and then summer, we have started riding together more often. Sometimes we head out with the local club, other times just the two of us. Our lives have also assumed a rhythm, something we never had while I was racing. That is comforting. We take the boys to school, we work during the day, and we pick them up in the late afternoon. We spend Saturdays and Sundays together, as a family. We ride for fun and fitness. There are no longer finish lines or cheering fans. But that doesn't seem to matter.

On the dirt road, we chat, then breathe hard on the climbs. We push each other just enough but not too much. The gravel road turns to tarmac, an abrupt transition in friction and impact that makes the bike feel as if it could suddenly sail along alone. We can hear the hum of car tyres in the distance. Buildings appear with increasing frequency along the roadside. Descending again, the road becomes congested with cars, houses, flags, mailboxes, dogs and garbage cans. We freewheel down to the port, an idyllic spot where tourists photograph the lake, each other and the boats.

We both know we'll stop to get a drink and a pastry or something. This time, we buy waffle cones loaded with ice cream and devour them while sitting on a dock.

As Dede calls my parents, to check in with them and to see how the boys are doing – I hear they've caught half a dozen fish – I think for a moment about the last year, as I have done so often since I testified and retired. I think about my career, the life I've spent on a bike, and how it is still such an integral part of who I am, no matter how many times I've wanted to give it up, been angry at it and even hated it.

I gaze into the lake and my reflection in the water: the logo-free cycling clothing, the buckled helmet, the glasses covering my eyes, and my clean-shaven legs. I am no longer paid to ride. I reflect on the wrong I have done, how deeply I regret the decision I made, and most of all, how I betrayed those who supported me. Admitting to cheating and being confronted with my past was not only the hardest experience of my life, it also enriched me in ways I could never have imagined. It has given me greater perspective on what I did, how I ended up crossing a line I swore I never would.

To satisfy my ego, I gave in to, and fed, a culture that ultimately devoured the childhood dreams that were once so pure and innocent. Racing, and the business it is, ate at me and consumed me in many ways. But riding has also provided moments of reflection, clarity, sanctity, as it has in the last months.

I retired knowing cycling is now in a better state as a result of the changes that have occurred since 2006. Because of improved testing and increasing intolerance of banned substances, riders can now win the toughest races without drugs. The sport has become more humane, but the evolution must continue. Most of the images in my dreams have now become reality. There are many teams committed to racing clean, respecting their riders and providing proper care. Most importantly, my hope is that through our experiences, the health of riders in future generations will take priority over their performance. But more needs to be done if cycling is to fully shake off its past. Cycling must create a culture in which riders, staff and officials no longer fear speaking the truth. When that happens, real reforms will follow.

And, despite its scars, cycling continues to flourish. The streets are filled with commuters, and cyclists participate in group rides in record numbers. Crowds at bike races fervently cheer on the passing riders. This testifies to the lasting beauty of the sport. Cycling is a people's sport, free to watch on a mountainside or a street corner. It evokes images of courage and youth. It brings us all back to our childhood, when we took our first pedal strokes and felt as if we were flying and free. We can revive that feeling every time we get on a bike.

Sitting on the dock in Muskoka, midway through a long ride, I can still see and feel the pure joy of cycling and of sport. I listen to Dede as she chats. I hear that childlike joy in her voice. The ride has given her that: discovering, sweating, feeling, breathing and moving. Even if only for a few hours, we've both become kids again.

ACKNOWLEDGEMENTS

Thank you to Mr Webb, my high school English teacher, for instilling the importance of sitting down with a pen and paper for a few moments each day. In your class, I began writing about the places I discovered on my bike, the relationships I developed and the emotions I experienced. The scribbles I've accumulated over the years are the guts of this book.

To my parents, Mike and Clare, who introduced me to sport when I was a young boy, who shared my dream and supported me through my highest and lowest points. Since, my retirement, I now understand my life on a bike better than ever. Thank you Mom, Dad and Dede, for helping me to rediscover the love I have for the bike, for helping to understand how I lost it, and for helping me comprehend the true meaning of the ride. Thank you to the three of you for reading draft after draft of the manuscript; I know how difficult and heartbreaking it was for you to digest. Thank you Dede for your love, strength, patience and resilience. The bike brought us together, it tore at us, and then helped us rebuild. To Liam and Ashlin for giving me perspective when I needed it most.

Thanks to Ian Austen and Bruce MacDougall for always encouraging me to write, for teaching me, for providing thoughtful advice while reading over the manuscript and for being good friends through some of the toughest moments. Thanks to my friends Brendan Quirk, Tim Buckley, and Ian Auld for reading and advising. David Luxton, thank you for your guidance, for believing in this book and for keeping me on track.

Angus Cargill and Kate Ward of Faber & Faber, thank you for your patience. You did a brilliant job cleaning up and sorting out all of my messy drafts.

Thank you to my teammates and training partners for the shared memories; it has been a tumultuous but maturing ride. Thanks to all of those who supported me from the roadside, over the airwaves, and in person – your encouragement held me together when I was about to crumble and was rocket fuel when I was in flight.

Michael Barry, February 2014

INDEX